CHILD
of Promise

by Debbi Migit

CHILD
of Promise

A True Story of Adoption:
One family's miraculous journey

TATE PUBLISHING & Enterprises

Published by Tate Publishing & Enterprises, LLC
127 E. Trade Center Terrace | Mustang, Oklahoma 73064 USA
1.888.361.9473 | www.tatepublishing.com

Tate Publishing is committed to excellence in the publishing industry. The company reflects the philosophy established by the founders, based on Psalm 68:11,
"The Lord gave the word and great was the company of those who published it."

Book design copyright © 2008 by Tate Publishing, LLC. All rights reserved.
Cover design by Jacob Crissup
Interior design by Kandi Evans

Published in the United States of America

ISBN: 978-1-60462-884-5
1. Family & Relationships: Adoption
2. Church & Ministry: Church Life
08.05.05

Dedication

To the memory of my dad, Paul E. Campbell, who taught me to believe in miracles.

And to the memory of my twin brother, Dave Campbell, who taught me to hear the harmony.

Acknowledgements

I want to thank my mom, Bobbi Campbell, for modeling the ministry of motherhood with unconditional love, laughter, and a bit of Irish lace.

A very special "thank you" to my husband, Phil. I wouldn't want to make this journey with anyone else!

And of course, my three beautiful children, Alex, Ethan, and Kate, each one a true Child of Promise.

I also thank my extended family for their encouragement, and my Trinity family for their oversight and support of Child of Promise Ministries.

A special thanks to my assistant, Jenny Thomas, and to Brenda Shaver, Lynnae Kellum, Jen Miller, Christine Phillips, and Connie Springer, for encouraging me to "write the book!"

I would like to thank David Lee of Photography by Lee, for my cover photo.

Finally, I thank Tate publishing for offering me the opportunity to "Publish His glorious deeds among the nations; tell everyone about the amazing things He does," (1 Chronicles 16:24, NLT).

Author Note

Child of Promise is the true account of our adoption miracles. I have tried to tell the story as accurately as memory allows, with some creative license taken for insignificant details. However, all of the miraculous events occurred as they are detailed in this story. I have a keen sense of responsibility to report the facts as they happened. We have an amazing God, and He doesn't need my help to prove it. I have changed the names of just a few people in the book, most especially the birthmothers of our children. Otherwise, all names, places, and dates are accurate.

A JEWISH PRAYER:

We did not plant you,
True.
But when the season is done,
When alternate prayers
For sun and rain are counted,
When the pain of weeding
And the pride of watching are through,
We will hold you high.
A shining leaf
Above the thousand seeds grown wild.
Not by our planting,
But by heaven
Our harvest.
Our child.
-Author unknown-

Chapter One

CHRISTMAS EVE 1986

I was pregnant. Wrapping my arms around my tummy, I hugged the sweet knowledge to myself. I imagined I could even feel a fluttering inside, although I knew that was impossible. It was too soon, of course. I squirmed in my seat like a ten-year-old about to enter Disneyland. The woman sitting on the opposite side of the waiting room darted a glance up from her magazine, and I willed myself to be composed. She looked about twenty-five-years-old, and she was very pregnant. For a moment I felt a famil-iar twinge of jealousy, but quickly pushed it away. The old patterns would need to change. If I was truly pregnant, I would finally be able to look at other mommies-to-be and feel a sense of kinship instead of sadness or anger. Joy simmered, and I gave the woman a companionable smile. Casually crossing my legs, I smoothed my navy slacks, brushing off a spot of salt that lingered from my walk through the slush outside. My navy shoes were soaked, a testament to my reluctance to wear boots. Although I had lived in Illinois all of my life, I had a stubborn resistance to wearing winter clothing. It had been snowing for hours, and the road crews were working overtime to make sure everyone could make it home for the holidays. Another wave of excitement shivered through me. *Pregnant, and on Christmas Eve, no less! It's perfect.* My lips curved in an irrepressible grin. Eight years of pain began to melt away. The infertility tests, miscarriages and grief were now overshadowed by the joy of the moment. All that was important was that tonight I would be giving my husband the gift of a lifetime.

On the floor next to me, a little girl rummaged through the meager contents of a toy box. Blocks quickly littered the floor as she dug deep for her prize. I smiled as I watched her pull out a stuffed green frog and give it a hug. *What was the frog's name?* I realized that I would soon be very familiar with the frog and many other characters. But I was a traditionalist; visions of a nursery inhabited by Pooh and his friends teased my mind.

It was 2:00 p.m. and Dr. Shay's office was nearly empty. On the other side of the reception desk I could see the nurses, Janet and Chris, as they took a moment from their work to sample the apple cake that a patient had brought in to the office. They had offered me a piece earlier, but I was too excited to eat, although the spicy aroma that still lingered from the cake was a nice treat. The window around the desk was decorated, and Christmas lights blinked, causing the silver garland to sparkle. I couldn't imagine a better setting to finally receive the positive news of my pregnancy.

Down the hall a door opened, then closed, and I heard Dr. Shay's voice as he spoke to Janet. After eight years of battling infertility, Dr. Shay, Janet, and Chris had become almost like family in my mind. When Dr. Shay had examined me a few moments earlier, it seemed he was as excited as I was when he announced, "It looks like the Clomid finally did the trick!" What he didn't say was, "It's a good thing, too." I knew that if I hadn't become pregnant this time, we would have to try another method. Because of the long term side effects, six months of Clomid was all I was allowed. My husband, Phil, had been a little wary of the Clomid from the beginning. The stories of multiple births worried him, although I explained that other drugs were more likely to bring that result. "Did you remind the doctor that you are a twin, and that twins run in your family?" Phil had cautioned. "Tell him we want a baby, not a litter!" We had both laughed, but I knew that Phil was still uncertain about having one baby, let alone two. Since my grandmother was a twin, and two of her eight children had produced twins, I could understand Phil's caution. I had dreamed of having several children, and now, at age thirty-one, time was getting short. Caught up in the magic of the moment, I allowed myself a brief hope that I really might be carrying twins.

Dr. Shay's voice was muffled as he moved down the hall. I nervously picked up a magazine and tried to distract myself. Janet had taken my blood test and asked me to stay in the waiting room for a few minutes while they confirmed my pregnancy. A toothless baby grinned up at me from the cover of a magazine. When I had first come to see Dr. Shay, I poured over the parenting magazines in his waiting room, soaking up every bit of wit and wisdom they offered. After the first year, though, I'd studiously begun to avoid them in favor of more generic reading material. But today I quickly thumbed through the pages, hoping to catch up. There was so much to learn.

"Debbi?" Janet leaned around the door frame. "Dr. Shay can see you now." I carefully replaced the magazine and followed Janet to the private office Phil and I had visited once, so many years ago. I tried to picture how Dr. Shay would officially announce my pregnancy. One time, about four years earlier, I had been waiting in an exam room when I heard Dr. Shay enter the room next door. His booming voice came through as he announced to the patient, "Congratulations lady. You are pregnant!" Tears suddenly clogged my throat at that memory, and the years of longing to hear those words.

For eight years, Phil and I had faced the pain of infertility, and my faith had been shaken to its foundation. Although my life had been marked by miracles, including being healed of a terminal illness, I struggled to understand why we were being denied the blessing of children. But now, finally, I would have the desire of my heart. My pulse quickened as I heard Dr. Shay's knock at the door.

"Come in!" I responded, trying to appear calm. Any second now, the doctor would deliver the wonderful news...I had no idea that a few hours later, God would begin a new adventure in our lives that would change everything.

Chapter Two

MAY, 1962

I was dying. Since I was only seven-years-old, I didn't have a firm grasp of what that meant, but I sensed it wasn't good. The nagging cough that kept me up nights had prompted my parents to take me to the doctor, who in turn sent us straight to the hospital. The diagnosis sounded like a foreign language to me—hystoplasmosis. The doctors weren't sure if I had contracted the disease from the old tree stump where I sat every day waiting for the school bus, or possibly from our pet parakeet. The doctors explained to my parents that the disease had caused a fungus to grow on the outside of my lungs. There was no cure.

At the hospital, I had a semi-private room, which was strange, since I had shared a room with my twin brother, Dave, since before we were born. Because the hospital was over thirty miles from our home, my parents weren't able to stay with me all of the time. So, when the nurses brought a little girl in to fill the next bed, I was excited. Her name was Sarah. She was about my age and very friendly. Within minutes we were chatting and giggling, and I decided the hospital wasn't such a bad place after all. About a half hour later, Sarah's mom hurried to her bedside.

"Honey, would you like me to go downstairs and get us both a milkshake?" Sarah nodded and said, "Thanks, Mommy; could Debbi have one, too?" Sarah's mom glanced at me and I saw her hesitate before answering. "Well, honey, I'm not sure if that is okay with Debbi's doctor."

Before I could respond that I was sure my doctor would be delighted for me, Sarah's mom hurried out, returning a few moments later with two chocolate shakes. Sarah hesitated, then obeyed her mother's prompting and began to drink. For a few moments the room was quiet, except for the sound of Sarah and her mom slurping their shakes. Just as they finished their treat, Nurse Patty came in and Sarah's mom pointed at me.

"I wasn't sure if Debbi could have a shake or not," she said defensively. The nurse frowned and said, "Actually, Debbi doesn't have any dietary restrictions. If you'd stopped at the desk I could have explained that to you." Nurse Patty came over to fluff my pillow and from the look she gave me I thought I could expect an extra pudding on my tray that evening.

As the nurse left the room, Sarah's mom followed her out the door and I heard her ask, "Is Debbi contagious?" I couldn't hear the reply and I wasn't sure what contagious meant, but it must not have been good because two hours later, Sarah was moved to a different room and I was alone again.

There was only one television in the children's wing, and on Saturdays we were all herded down to sit in the play room and watch *Sky King* and *My Friend, Flicka*. I loved to pretend that I was Penny, Sky King's niece. Penny wasn't afraid of anything.

After two weeks in the hospital I was released to go home, but if I thought life would return to normal, I was wrong. My family lived in Midway, which came by its name honestly. It was, well, midway, between Pekin and South Pekin. Our home was small, but neat as a pin. My mother loved to decorate and try new furniture arrangements. There was more than one evening when my dad came home late from duty in the Air Force Reserves, to find that Mom had moved the furniture while he was gone. In the dark I would hear him stumble into a piece of furniture that hadn't been there when he had left that morning. "I swear, I'm gonna nail that couch to the floor," he would say. I giggled into my pillow, knowing that in the morning Dad would tease Mom about the bruises on his shins.

My parents teased each other a lot. I only heard them argue one time, just before I got sick, and I was the cause. Actually, it had been Dave's fault. Since Dave had been born twelve minutes before me, he considered himself the older brother and he liked to tease me. One day he took a motor boat that had a wind-up crank on the bottom and he wound it as tight as he could. Then he put the boat against the back of my hair and let the crank go. My hair was my mom's pride and joy. She spent hours combing the thick, blonde locks into banana curls that hung halfway down my back. When the crank began to turn, it wound my hair up so tightly that there was no solution but to cut it off. My mom took me next door to our neighbor, Elsie, who ran a beauty shop on her back porch.

"Oh, poor baby, what happened?" Elsie scooted me up on the special booster seat she had made from coffee cans covered in upholstery material. It wasn't very comfortable, but at least I could see myself in the mirror. From the front I looked the same: blue eyes and blonde bangs that were cut high on my forehead. Two banana curls hung down on each side of my face like blonde sausages. But, when I turned my head, I could see the red motor boat that was docked there. I turned to glare at Dave who had followed us to Elsie's. He looked guilty and just a little scared. Good.

"Nothing to do but give her a pixie." Elsie picked up her scissors and started toward me.

"Wait!" My mom gently tried to pull the boat loose and I winced.

"Roberta, the hair has to be cut off. And pixies are really popular right now. She'll be right in style, you'll see." I squirmed as Elsie loosed the boat from its moorings and it clattered to the floor. My mom whimpered as she watched my banana curls fall, one by one, to form a pile of blonde hair on the floor. When Elsie was finished, my hair was a soft bob, not much longer than Dave's. We walked back home without a word and waited for Dad to come home from work. Dad was brokenhearted that I had lost my beautiful hair and he just couldn't understand that there had been no other solution. Mom tried to put a good light on it, telling him how much easier it would be to get me ready for church on Sundays, and reminding him that, of course, it would grow back. Eventually it did, but I never had banana curls again. Even though it wasn't my fault, I felt guilty that my parents were arguing. I'm not sure what Dave felt, other than a keen sense of the loss of his motorboat.

My parents met when my dad's brother, Chuck, married my mom's sister, Bonnie. My mom had told me that Chuck and Bonnie's boys were our "double cousins", since they were Flynn cousins and Campbell cousins. Chuck and Bonnie and the "doubles" had moved to Phoenix the previous year, and now we lived in their old house. My dad worked as an insurance salesman, and on the week-ends he served in the Air Force Reserves. I loved seeing my dad in his Air Force uniform. He was a sergeant and it seemed that every few months he would bring home new stripes for my mom to sew on his uniform. My mom always said, "You get the promotions, and I'll keep sewing." We had all lived on Scott Air Force base when Dave and I were younger, until my dad left active duty. I didn't remember the base, but I liked to look at the pictures my mom kept in an old album. My favorite was one of my dad, standing next to his bunk in the barracks. He was so slim and had a thin moustache. His hat was cocked back on his head and he was pointing to a picture of my mom that held a place of honor over the bunk.

My mom was beautiful. She had long, wavy hair that had some auburn highlights. Her eyes were bright blue. In the picture, her head was tilted back and she was laughing a little. I thought she looked just like a movie star I had seen on television named Maureen O'Hara. I figured since they were both Irish, they might even be cousins. All of the pictures in the album showed my parents smiling or laughing, and that didn't surprise me, since they laughed a lot in person, too. Since I had come home from the hospital, I hadn't seen them laugh as much any more.

I was restricted to lying on the couch all day. Any movement could aggravate my lungs and cause the disease to progress even more rapidly. My days settled into a pattern of watching Dave, and my best friend Connie, as they played outside.

Connie was a year older than we were, and she lived across the street in a two story Cape Cod that was the largest house in the neighborhood. As the youngest child in the family, Connie was the only one left at home and she always had the latest toys. She had just received a brand new bike that summer, and every morning I would push the lace curtains back so I could watch her fly down the road on her pink Schwinn. Just before I became ill, my parents had given Dave and me a used bicycle to share, and I watched Dave learn how to ride that summer. One day my mom had an inspiration, and she hooked the handlebars of the bike through the chain link fence and let me sit on the seat and pedal in place. I closed my eyes and pretended I was flying along the road like I had seen Dave and Connie doing. I tried to muffle any coughing, since that would bring my mom running to take me back inside.

My other joy was reading. Every week mom would visit the library in Pekin and come home loaded down with books for me to read. I especially loved a series of books about twins from all around the world. The twins were always boy/girl, just like Dave and me, and my cousins, Lisa and Lindsay. My favorite of the series was the story of African American twins. I asked my mom to bring that book home almost every single week. I had just finished first grade, and by the end of the summer I was reading at eighth grade level and beyond. I also kept a notebook close by to jot down stories and poems as they came to me. It was during that summer that I wrote my first worship song.

A few months earlier, my family had attended the Assemblies of God camp meeting in Petersburg, Illinois and, while we were there, I had accepted Jesus. It had rained most of the week-end and mud was everywhere, including in the big tent where the meeting was being held. Sawdust was scattered over the ground to cut down on the mess, but it didn't help much. I didn't care, though. One evening as the crowd sang, "*Into my heart, into my heart, come into my heart Lord Jesus,*" I walked through the sawdust to kneel in the mud, at the front, and ask Jesus into my heart. Now the forced solitude of my illness caused me to spend a lot of time talking to my new 'best friend'. When He began to talk back, I just assumed that was the way it was for everyone.

I loved it when I had visitors. My Sunday school teacher, Eileen Magner, often stopped by and brought me little gifts and trinkets. My parent's best friends, Marlene and Carroll Phillips, were regular visitors at the hospital and at our home. But best of all was when our pastor, Brother Richeson, came to pray for me. Brother Richeson was big, with a booming voice, especially when he started preaching. I always felt like I was standing next to God when he visited. A lot of people stopped at our home over that summer to visit and offer prayers for my healing. But, it wasn't until August that I began to understand just how sick I really was.

"Honey, you know school will be starting in a few weeks," my dad stated as he sat next to me on the couch.

I looked up from my book and said, "I know, I can't wait! Mrs. Armstrong is going to be my teacher this year. She is so nice!"

"Well, actually, you are going to have a different teacher. We will be getting a tutor to come here and you can go to school right here at home!" My mom tried to make it sound like an adventure, but I knew better. I had spent the summer watching my twin and my friends playing without me. Now I would have to watch them go off to school without me, too. It wasn't fair!

"Please, let me go to school," I begged. "I'll sit very quietly and not run, I promise."

"I'm sorry, honey." My mom knew how much I loved school and I could see her fighting back the tears. "The doctor said it is too risky. You have to stay quiet, remember?"

I slumped back against the couch. I tried to think of anything I might have done in my seven years that could cause me to be in this much trouble. First, I had been declared 'contagious' at the hospital, which kept me isolated from the other children. Now I couldn't even go to school with my brother and my friends. I began to feel like my disease made me dirty, somehow, and not good enough to be around other people. I tried to think of ways to make myself better; maybe if I was really good the doctor would change his mind.

At some point I must have realized that I was dying. One day I stunned my parents by suggesting calmly, "Remember that stuffed owl that we saw at the zoo last year? Well, how about when I die, maybe you can have me stuffed and I can sit in the corner and you won't miss me so much!" I thought this was a great solution, but the stricken look on my mom's face told me otherwise.

It was the week before school when I had a doctor's appointment to check the progress of the disease. I could sense my parents' fear as the doctor told them that he was ordering a new X-ray and that we should go to the hospital right away. I was used to the x-rays by now, so I was surprised when they took several more than usual. A few moments later the doctor called my parents back to his office while I sat in the waiting room and read my book. When my mom and dad came out of the office, they were smiling. And when we got in the car to go to my grandparent's house to pick up Dave, they gave me the good news.

"Baby, do you remember how all of our friends and Brother Richeson have been stopping by to pray for you?" My dad looked over his shoulder at me as he maneuvered the car out of the parking lot. I nodded; I could almost smell the scent of the special oil Bother Richeson would put on my forehead when he prayed for me.

"Well, God heard all those prayers," my mom said softly. "The doctor said that the hystoplasmosis is gone. You can even start school on time with Dave!" My mind raced. I was healed! I wasn't sure exactly what that meant, so I asked, "Can I take the bike out of the fence and ride it now?"

My parents laughed and explained, "You will need to have x-rays in a few months to make sure you are doing okay, but eventually you can do everything you used to do, including riding your bike." There was more excitement when we stopped at my grandparents and my mom and dad explained what the doctor had said. Grandma and Grandpa Flynn lived in a farm house in the country, and I gazed longingly at the big tire swing that hung from the oak tree. Dave and I loved to climb on the swing with our cousins and see how many of us could fit; at one time there were ten Flynn cousins swinging together. Now I could swing again, too.

"We have to get going," my mom told Grandma. "We are going to take the whole family to church tonight, for the first time in three months!"

Church! As soon as we got home, I ran in to get ready. I hadn't been to church, or anywhere but the doctor's office, in three months. My hands shook as I thought about all the friends I would see. I loved it when my dad led the congregation in singing hymns—I had missed it so much.

I was a little disappointed when we got to church and I realized we were late. Now I would have to wait until after the service to visit with my friends. Bother Richeson was standing at the pulpit as my family walked through the swinging doors, into the sanctuary, and I heard him say, "And here they are now!" A collective gasp went up from the congregation as they all stood and began to applaud. I looked around to see what the excitement was all about as my mom led Dave and me to a pew. My dad walked up to the stage and stood beside the pastor. I noticed people were crying and I was confused; were they happy or sad?

Finally the clapping stopped as my dad approached the microphone.

"I have a testimony tonight," he said in his deep voice. "The X-rays today confirmed that the disease is gone. Debbi has been healed!" As my dad and the musicians began to lead the congregation in worship, I looked around at all of the people who loved me and my family, and had prayed for me all these months. I wouldn't understand until many years later that God had given me two gifts that summer. One was my healing. The other: Faith.

Chapter Three

Over the next ten years, God began to train me in the art of hearing His voice. At times, it was something as simple as turning my Bible to the chapter Brother Richeson was going to preach from before he even came to the pulpit. Other times it was more serious. I learned that hearing and obeying could mean the difference between life and death.

Grandpa Campbell came to live with us when I was eighteen-years-old. My dad had told me once that Grandpa had been an itinerate preacher years earlier. He had traveled by horseback from town to town, preaching all over Arkansas and Missouri. He still preached occasionally, down at the Pentecostal church he attended. I loved my grandfather, but I thought he must miss preaching because he could launch into a sermon at the drop of a hat.

The years since my illness had been pretty quiet, with the exception of the birth of our brother, Scott, when Dave and I were eleven years old. Not long after Scott was born, we moved to Pekin, and now we lived in a large, two story home. My mom had many more rooms to redecorate and she loved every minute.

Dave had recently left to attend North Central Bible College in Minnesota. One week-end, my parents decided to visit him, and they asked me to check on Grandpa some time during the evening.

"He will most likely be asleep when you stop in after the concert, but just look in on him before you go on to Lora's party, okay?" My mom was trying to finish packing Scott's clothes for the trip.

The 'asleep' part sounded good to me, since Grandpa was a non-stop talker when he was awake. I had lost count of the times I was late to meet my friends because Grandpa decided to tell me about his years as a brick layer, or what life had been like during the Great Depression. I some-times wondered why he wanted to talk about it so much if it had been so depressing.

When my friend, Lora, and I slipped into the house that night, we purposely left the lights off. As we tiptoed into the kitchen, I asked Lora to grab some snacks while I ran upstairs to check on Grandpa.

"Shh," I whispered. "We have to be very quiet. If we wake him up, we'll never get to the party."

I started toward the stairway and cautiously put my foot on the first step. I knew most of the creaks in the old wood floor, but sometimes one would surprise me; I wasn't in the mood for surprises tonight. The Christian concert had been great, and now we were headed back to Lora's house to hang out with some friends from church. At sixteen, Lora was the youngest of our group, and she was eager to get the party started. I had asked her to ride with me to check on Grandpa, and now I didn't want to hold her up any more.

The first step was quiet and I relaxed a bit. The second step creaked a little and after the small noise I held my breath and listened. The silence reassured me and I started to go up to the next step.

Suddenly I heard a soft voice whisper to my heart, "*Call out to your Grandfather.*" I paused with my foot in midair. *Where had that thought come from?* I put my foot down and stepped up. Another small creak sounded in the stillness and then there was silence.

I took another step and the voice was clearer this time. "*Call out his name!*"

After a moment's hesitation I called softly, "Grandpa?" Immediately Lora appeared at the bottom of the stairs.

"Are you nuts? Please, please don't wake him up!" Lora loved my Grandpa, but Tim O'Donnell was going to be at the party. There was just no contest.

"I can't help it," I whispered back. "I have to do this." I took another step up and this time my legs felt like lead.

"*Call out to your Grandfather!*" The voice was so loud in my mind that I turned to look at Lora, certain that she had heard it, too. Lora continued to watch me with a mutinous expression and I gave a helpless shrug before turning back to call out again—loudly this time.

"Grandpa! It's Debbi. Everything is ok." The landing at the top of the stairs was bathed in moonlight and I watched in dismay as my grandfather stepped out of the shadows and stood silhouetted in the faint light. The next moment felt like a lifetime as I stared at the barrel of his gun.

"Debbi, is that you?" I held my breath as Grandpa's shaking hand lowered the gun, then trembling, I ran up the stairs to him.

"It's okay," I said as he began to weep.

"Sweetheart, I almost killed you. What was I thinking?" Gently taking the gun from him, I put it out of reach until my dad returned and could unload it.

"Debbi, I heard you at the door and I thought it was someone trying to break into the house. Then, when the lights didn't come on and you were whispering, I was sure it was a burglar, so I grabbed my gun and loaded it. Honey, my finger was on the trigger and I was going to fire on the next step. How did you know I was up here?"

"I didn't," I explained softly. "God did, and He told me to call out your name. I just obeyed."

"Thank God," Grandpa said, as he hugged me close.

"Yes," I whispered, as I thought about my initial refusal to obey that still small voice. "Thank God."

I often thought of that night when I heard God's whispers to my heart, and as frightening as it had been, I always appreciated the lesson it carried. Hearing and obeying God's voice would need to become a priority in my life in the days ahead. But although I was progressing in the hearing part, obeying was not always as easy, and sometimes others had to pay the price for my disobedience.

The dream woke me again and I tried to shake off the uneasiness I felt. I had been having this same dream for days now, and I was exhausted. Finally, one morning I couldn't keep it in any longer.

"I'm worried about Joanie." Pouring milk into my tea, I sat at the kitchen table, across from my mom. "I keep having dreams that something bad is going to happen to her. I think she might even die." Although Joanie Parker was two years younger than I, we had been friends since we were children growing up together in church. But recently, Joanie had started dating a guy who was much older and she never came to church anymore.

"Well, we will pray and then trust God to protect Joanie," my mom answered calmly. I could tell she was concerned about me, too, because I hadn't slept well since the dreams started.

A few weeks later I was excited to see Joanie walk into Sunday School class. Although she sat by herself, I hoped it meant that God was answering my prayers. As soon as class was dismissed, I followed Joanie to the water fountain located in the church basement.

"Hi, I've missed you!" I greeted Joanie as she turned from the fountain. The coldness in her eyes surprised me, but I continued. "How have you been?"

"Busy." The curt answer made me hesitate for just a moment.

"Well, the youth group is having a wiener roast tonight, why don't you join us?" I followed as Joanie turned and began to climb the stairs that led to the foyer.

"I have plans," Joanie said.

I raced to catch up as she moved quickly toward the sanctuary doors.

"Joanie." I touched her arm lightly but she shrugged me off.

"Look, I'm only here for the next two weeks to say good-bye to Brother and Sister Richeson. You can tell my parents you did what they asked and invited me to join you. I'm sure they won't blame you that I said 'no'."

The last part was said with a sneer and I pulled away, hurt.

"They want me to be like you—a goody-two-shoes. Forget it, and leave me alone!" Joanie pushed through the doors and slumped in the back pew.

The following week, Brother and Sister Richeson were retiring from the ministry. After twenty years as the pastors of First Assembly of God Church, they were going to move to the Assembly of God campgrounds in Carlinville. The church had planned a special celebration and it looked like anyone who had ever attended our church was at the party. My mom and her friend Marlene had spent weeks making mints and decorating, and now the fellowship hall was full of color, laughter, and even a few tears as we said good-bye to our pastors. I sat, enjoying turkey and dressing with Lora and our friend, Linda, as we planned for an afternoon at the Dragon Roller Rink. We decided that skating would be the perfect antidote to Marlene's delicious cheesecake.

"I'll go ask the "BURs" to join us." Linda nodded at Jerry and Randy, two of the guys from our youth group. Jerry and Randy had recently declared that they were 'Bachelors Until Rapture' and were now nicknamed the BURs. Linda seemed to take the BURs declaration personally, especially when it came from Jerry. As Linda headed for the guy's table, I noticed Joanie and her boyfriend, Troy, making their way through the buffet line. As I watched them carry their plastic dinner plates and find a seat, I heard that now familiar voice: *Invite Joanie to come skating this afternoon.* I immediately thought of my conversation with Joanie last week and the hurt stung again. Shrugging off the instruction, I moved to a table to visit with my friend, Fran, to plan our upcoming vacation. A few moments later I saw Joanie and Troy stand and move to throw away their plates. "See, God, they're leaving," I whispered in relief. I was off the hook.

"Go after them." With a sigh I dumped the rest of my cheesecake and headed for the door, slowly. Friends stopped me as I walked by, and I let myself be detained a little. I was obeying, just at my own pace, I rationalized. I stopped to talk to Linda; after all I needed the correct information on where we were all going, because I couldn't just invite Joanie and Troy along if I didn't have all the details. I finally made my way to the foyer, just in time to

see Troy's Harley pull out of the parking lot. I had missed them.

"I'm sorry, God," I whispered as I went back inside. "I promise, the next time I will ask her right away. Maybe I'll even call her this week and see if we can get together, just the two of us." That would be better, I reasoned, as I helped clean up the kitchen. I could talk to Joanie a lot easier without Troy along to distract her. I felt pretty good about my 'Plan B', and with a lighter heart I headed out to meet my friends.

The sirens seemed to explode around me as I walked to my car. A moment later an ambulance raced by, and I somehow knew: there might not be a next time for Joanie.

One of the young men from our church was working that day with the rescue squad. I heard later that as he helped care for Joanie, he didn't even recognize her, although he had known Joanie all of her life. Just two blocks from the party, a car had run a red light and hit Troy and Joanie on the motorcycle. The driver of the car was killed instantly. Troy had some minor injuries, but Joanie was in a coma and paralyzed. She wasn't expected to live.

The guilt was almost unbearable. Night after night I woke with nightmares as I dreamed about the accident. Although I had never met the woman who was killed, I saw her face every night. My parents thought I was upset about Joanie, and I was, but they had no idea about what had really happened that day. I just couldn't share that awful truth with anyone. Even the fact that Joanie was progressing better than the doctors had predicted didn't make any difference. She was still paralyzed, and was facing many surgeries. I began to be tormented, especially when I went to church and saw Joanie's parents weeping in prayer. I tried to pray, too, but I just couldn't imagine that God would forgive me for what I had done—or hadn't done.

One Sunday night the emotional pain became unbearable, and I left the service to find my favorite hiding place in the basement of the church. My dad found me there.

"You can't go on like this, you know," he said as he sat next to me. "Can you tell me what is wrong? Are you worried about Joanie?" I began to cry as I poured out the whole story to him. Then I waited for his condemnation.

"Oh, baby," my dad cried, too, as he gathered me in his arms. "I had no idea you were living with this. The accident was not your fault—and God doesn't blame you. Yes, He offered you the opportunity to speak to Joanie and you didn't take it, but God gave Joanie a free will and there is no assurance that if you had invited her, she would have gone with you that day, instead of with Troy. And the other driver, the woman who was killed, that wasn't your fault either. Even if Joanie hadn't been on the back of the bike, the accident would still have happened when the other woman ran the stop sign. She would have died either way. You have to find a way to forgive yourself, because God already has." As my dad prayed for me I felt the torment stop for the first time since the accident. I was surrounded by God's peace and I began to forgive myself for letting fear keep me from stepping out and speaking to Joanie that day. After a while, my dad and I went back up to the service, and I was able to enjoy the presence of the Lord for the first time in a long time.

Six months later, Joanie walked back into First Assembly. I felt a sense of deja vu as the entire congregation stood, weeping, and applauding. Once again, God had brought back one of their daughters from the edge of death. I could barely sit still during the service, and as the altar call was given my breath caught as I saw Joanie stand. But tears stung my eyes as I saw her turn and walk out of the sanctuary door.

Racing after her, I saw her disappear down the same back stairs where we'd had our last conversation. When I reached the bottom of the stairs, I saw Joanie at the water fountain and I knew that God was giving me a second chance. I just prayed that Joanie would accept hers, too. As she turned from the fountain, I gently touched her arm.

"Joanie. Please forgive me." Tears filled her eyes as she nodded, although I was sure she didn't know why I was apologizing. "Would you like to go up to pray?" I asked quietly. "I'll go with you." Joanie nodded again, and without a word we once again made the trip up the stairs, through the sanctuary doors, and down the center aisle. As we knelt together at the altar, I was overwhelmed by God's faithfulness, to us both. That night I made a promise to God. From that point on I was determined that if God ever again trusted me enough to ask something of me, I would have only one response: Obedience.

Chapter Four

The autumn of 1973 was decision time. I had recently graduated from high school; several of my closest friends were all leaving for North Central Bible College, and our pastor was encouraging me to go, too. I was still living at home and working full time at Waldenbooks in the local mall. Although I loved my job (I was surrounded by books!) I knew that if I was going to go on to school, this was the point of my life to take the step. But, I was so concerned about making a wrong decision that I couldn't seem to make any decision at all. The night before my friends were to leave, I attended a going-away-party at the home of our youth pastors, Gary and Bonnie Grogan.

"It's not too late; you can still enroll for the spring semester." Linda sat next to me on the couch. "We might even be in the same dorm."

"I'll pray about it," I promised, hugging her good-bye. Driving home later that evening, I popped in a cassette of Dallas Holmes singing what I had come to consider my theme song for the moment.

Which way do I turn and how do I learn what the Lord
wants me to do? I ask Him
His will and He says to be still and be sure that I'll lead
you through.
But I'm just a man, and I've got to know right now, which
way to go,
There are doors, opening for me, which one is the right
one for me?
Well I can't walk through two open doors—I can only
walk through one at a time,
There are doors that are opening for me—how do I know
which one is mine?

Dallas Holmes

As I sang along with Dallas, the words had never been
so real to me as at that moment. The music filled the car,
and tears began to fall as I sang again in a broken voice—
"which way do I turn?" I felt paralyzed by fear. *What if I
made a mistake and missed what God had planned for my life?*
Maybe I should quit my job tomorrow and take the risk,
praying that God would make it work. *But, what if His will
was for me to stay here, maybe even get married and start the
family I longed for. What if I missed that? Which way should
I turn?*

"*Turn right.*" Even with the music playing I had no
trouble hearing the words as the direction was given.

"*Turn right.*" Remarkably, I was nearing an intersection
and had been debating which road to take to go home.

Normally, I would go straight, since that seemed like the shortest route. But if I turned right, I would also arrive at my home—it would just take a little longer. I took a moment to wonder why God would respond so literally to my cry of "Which way do I turn?" Surely He knew what a metaphor was!

"*Turn right.*" I sat at the stop sign and considered my options. It was after midnight, and there was no other traffic around. My experiences in the previous years with my Grandpa and Joanie had taught me one thing. Even though I might not understand why, God was giving me a clear instruction; it was probably in my best interest to obey Him.

I turned right. The empty streets allowed me to drive slowly, and I scanned the area carefully, looking for something, anything, that would explain why I was on this road. Although a few lights flickered in living room windows, for the most part the neighborhood was asleep. My heart began to pound as I thought about the revelation I was about to receive. Surely God was going to tell me if I should quit my job and go to Bible college. Approaching another stop sign, I listened for a new direction to be given. Nothing. With a shrug I continued on the road I was traveling; apparently there was not going to be a running dialogue that would direct me. I was just going to follow the direction I had been given. As I neared my home, confusion began to replace my excitement. *Why hadn't God spoken to me again?* I pulled over to the side of the road and turned off the car. Replaying the experience, I considered that I might have avoided an accident by taking the route I had. If that was the case, I might never know why God had told me to turn right. But I became aware of a certainty in my heart. I had heard God's voice. And in the next moment He spoke again: "*Daughter, you can trust Me with your life and your decisions. Just as you recognized My voice tonight, you will come to know it even more as you grow in Me. Don't be afraid of 'missing' Me. I will direct your path.*"

Peace flooded my heart as I thought about what He had said. I knew that God had been training me for years to hear His voice. And as I settled my heart to listen, He spoke again. "*Don't make your life decisions based on fear; I have not given you a spirit of fear, but of power, love, and a sound mind. Don't let fear drive you, let My peace lead you.*" As I drove home that night I had no idea how many times in the years to come I would need to remember the anti-dote for fear: Peace.

Chapter Five

I met Jake on my first day as a secretary at Metropolitan Life Insurance Company. Six months had passed, and so had the deadline to apply for Bible college. But, peace had led me to stay home; now I had a new career and I was saving for my own apartment. I was anxious to see what was coming next, but I don't think anything could have prepared me for Jake Anderson.

Jake stopped by my desk and introduced himself. "So you're the new girl, huh?" His smile was partially hidden under a dark moustache; a lit cigar dangled from the corner of his mouth.

I wrinkled my nose at the smell, but answered politely, "Yes, is there something you need?"

"Actually I need a date for this week-end, how about it?" I looked closer to re-evaluate Jake. About twenty-three-years-old, business suit, nice looking, and—a cigar. Yuck.

"No thank you," I said and returned to my work.

That scene was repeated every single working day for six months. There was even an office bet started on when I would say 'yes'. The guys that worked with Jake were betting on him; all the secretaries had their money on me. After a few months, Jake changed his approach.

"Listen, I know you're a Christian. So am I." I glanced up from my typing to see Jake leaning on my desk. For the first time he was not smoking a cigar. "I'm not really as bad as you think. I bet I know the Bible even better than you do!" At my raised brow Jake proceeded to quote the entire chapter of Psalm 23. As if he sensed my thawing, Jake confided, "I was the captain of our Bible Brigade for two years running."

"How nice for you," I said with a grin.

"So, will you go out with me?" Jake apparently figured he had found the way to my heart by way of the Psalms.

"Thanks for asking," I answered. "But, I don't think so." Jake shrugged, and with a gleam in his eye promised he would be back tomorrow. I sighed as I watch him walk away. Really, I wished he would give up. I had sensed from the very beginning that Jake was not the person God had destined for me, and I didn't want to lead him on. I had plenty of friends, and I didn't want to begin a relationship that Jake obviously hoped would become more.

I held out for six whole months, until Jake finally decided to stop playing fair. One week-end when my parents were out of town, and I had the house to myself, the doorbell rang. I opened it to find Jake standing there with a fresh pizza and a grin. I sighed and let him in.

We dated for almost six months, and I was miserable for most of them. We argued often about the lines I had drawn regarding our physical relationship. Although Jake professed to be a Christian and even attended church with me at times, he made it known that he was not happy with my restrictions. I dreaded being with him, but in a strange way I dreaded being without him, too. I considered the possibility that I was supposed to help Jake in his relationship with God. I bristled at the term my friends used to describe our relationship: 'Missionary dating'. Unfortunately, I seemed to be the one being proselytized. I spent less time with my friends and my own interests, and more time just hanging out with Jake, mostly in front of the television. I was miserable, and it was becoming obvious. Finally, I could take it no longer, and I told Jake it was over.

I should have remembered Jake's determination from the beginning. Now he followed me everywhere I went and even trailed me on other dates. I often came out of work to find him going through my car and glove compartment. Several times I even found bouquets of dead flowers waiting for me on my car seat or door step. It was beginning to affect my work, and Jake's, too. Things came to a head one day when I heard that Jake had been fired for stalking me. I hoped that would be the end of it, but again, I misjudged Jake. He started to follow me home from work every day, trying to discover where my new apartment was located. I drove all over, trying to lose him, and then returned home to barricade myself behind the locked door. After several weeks, Jake finally tracked me down by having a friend at the office slip him my new address. He parked outside my apartment, watching me for hours. I was scared, but I hesitated to call the police since my dad now worked as a dispatcher for the police department. I knew that if he found out what Jake had been up to, Dad might damage his own career by confronting him.

One day Jake boldly walked into the office as I left work. "Hi there," he said, as if there was no break-up or a potential restraining order between us. "My car's in the shop; could you give me a ride home?" My initial reaction of, "No way!" was stopped as I thought about the possibility of putting an end to this craziness. Maybe all Jake needed was some closure.

"Okay, c'mon," I said ungraciously. My inner alarm began to sound as soon as we reached the car, and I almost turned to tell him I had changed my mind. But Jake reached around and held the car door for me and gave me an innocent smile. I thought, *What could happen?*

Plenty. As soon as I began to drive, the Holy Spirit spoke quietly to my heart. "*Jake is going to ask you to take him someplace where you are not familiar with the area. He wants to hurt you. Don't go anywhere but straight to his home.*" I glanced over at Jake, and tried to keep my expression passive.

Jake turned to look at me and said, "Hey, you can just drop me at my friend Bob's house. It's not too far out of town, okay?"

I shivered and turned back to my driving. I could feel

the hairs on the back of my neck begin to bristle as I realized what had just happened. If I hadn't had that warning a split second before he spoke, I would have agreed with Jake's request.

"Sorry," I said. "I can only go as far as your parent's house today. Take it or leave it." Jake glared at me for a moment and then tried again. As he realized I was not budging, I could tell he was becoming angry. We made the rest of the drive in silence and I abandoned my hope of having a rational discussion. As we neared his street, Jake said, "Turn here, my parent's road has construction on it." Since we were only a few blocks from his home, and I was familiar with the area, I did as he asked. Suddenly, Jake grabbed my arm and pointed up ahead to a house on the right. "Pull over here."

I pulled away and said, "If I stop, you get out." Under my breath I began to pray for God's protection as I saw the look in his eyes and realized that in the past weeks Jake's professed love for me had turned to hate. After a tense moment, Jake moved away and stared at the house he had indicated. As we passed, I saw that it was abandoned and most of the windows were broken. I turned a startled look to Jake and he gave me a strange smile.

"Well, maybe I can take you there another day," Jake promised. "It's a very—interesting house. My friend John died there." My heart pounded in my throat as I sensed the absolute presence of evil sitting next to me. With relief I spotted Jake's house and turned the car into the driveway.

"Get out now, and don't follow me anymore, or I will call the police." Jake glared at me for another second, and then he climbed out of the car without another word.

The following day I spoke to one of the agents that had stayed in touch with Jake. As I confided to Mark what Jake was doing, he assured me that he would speak to him and make sure Jake left me alone. For a time that seemed to help, and soon my days settled back to normal.

It was the week before Christmas, and I had one more gift to purchase. My dad had admired a new type of necktie that zipped on, and only one store in the area carried it. Unfortunately, that store was in the same town where Jake lived. I hadn't even driven into his town since that day, and I tried to bolster my courage as I quickly did my shopping and then stopped at a nearby hamburger place for dinner. I continued to remind myself that I had told no one where I was headed. There was no way Jake could know I was in town. The restaurant had big picture windows, and I tried to hide behind other customers as I waited to place my order. I couldn't shake the feeling of being exposed. Continuing to chide myself for my fear, I took my meal and went to the car.

"Get a grip," I spoke out loud as I turned to take my sandwich from the bag. "What are the chances that Jake would see me in that very window at that very moment?" I shrugged off the uneasy feeling and dug out a French fry. Starting the car, I turned to look out the window to back out of the parking place- and stared right at Jake, sitting in his car. He sat with his arm draped across the back of his seat, just watching me. He must have pulled into the empty space next to my car when I turned to put my food down. Even in the darkness, I could see the hatred gleaming in his eyes, and I reached up to hit the door lock. I pulled out of the lot and took off with Jake in pursuit. I was at a disadvantage since I didn't know Jake's hometown well, and he did. Scanning the oncoming cars, I searched for a police officer, but none appeared. Racing up and down the streets, I tried to lose Jake without becoming lost myself. Finally, I spotted a church parking lot that was filled with cars and people and quickly pulled up to the front door. Jake drove on by, honking madly as I sat shaking.

Heading home, I was thankful for another weapon in my Father's arsenal: Protection.

Chapter Six

"Phil Migit sounds like a jerk." I tried to take the sting out of my words with a smile, but still, I thought they needed to be said. My new friend Trisha shook her head in denial.

"No, really, he's a great guy. I think maybe I didn't explain him very well." Trisha had spent the last two weeks telling me about her failed relationship with her ex-fiancé. Apparently, he was moving back to town and she wanted another chance with him. "I was hoping you might help me with a make-over. I want him to see a new Trisha when he comes home."

I thought the old Trisha was pretty great already. I was especially impressed that Trisha had already been through nursing school and was working at the local hospital. Although I still had doubts about whether Phil deserved her, my romantic soul quickly became caught up in her plan.

Over the next few weeks I accompanied Trisha on shopping expeditions and hair appointments. All the while I continued to quiz her on what Phil was like, hoping to see if we could discover why he had broken the engagement in the first place.

"Well, first of all, he's very smart." Trisha set down her purchases as we took a break from our shopping to have some lunch. She actually glowed as she described her mystery man. "He has a genius IQ, and was going to be a teacher until he got into the auto body business." Trisha reached for the sugar packet and slowly stirred her coffee. "You know, I've been thinking that maybe that was the problem between us. Phil has some very definite ideas about so many things, and he isn't shy about expressing them, but I'm not really interested in politics and world events like he is, so we don't always have a lot to talk about. Mostly I just smile and nod in agreement."

"Well, we can work on that, too." I assured her. Secretly, however, I continued to be concerned about the success of our plan. The more I learned about Phil, the less I liked him, and in one of my more honest moments I was tempted to tell Trisha, "You know, maybe God saved you a lot of grief when you two broke up." One problem, at least in my viewpoint, was that he apparently was very logical and rather unemotional.

"Phil admires Spock." Trisha confided.

"Doctor or Mr.?" I asked. Trisha looked confused for a moment and then laughed.

"Mr. Spock," she replied, wrinkling her nose. I assumed that meant she wasn't a fan of the science fiction series, Star Trek, and I decided not to share my enthusiasm for the program. Although I found Mr. Spock intriguing, I was a Captain Kirk girl, myself.

Trisha had introduced me to another old friend of Phil's, and now Randy joined us as we gathered our energy for another bout of shopping. Randy had also filled in some of the blanks about Phil's opinions. Their conversations were filled with statements such as "Phil doesn't like this," or, "I wouldn't want to buy that, Phil would hate it!" As the day wore on I became so exasperated by Phil's opinions (he wasn't even in the state yet!) that I walked over to a mannequin and pointed to the blouse on display.

"Would Phil like this?" I asked innocently. Randy and Trisha both gaped at me. The psychedelic print was really not my favorite, either, but I was feeling a little rebellious.

"No way," Randy shook his head. "Phil hates that style."

"Great," I said. "I'm buying it." Trisha looked around nervously, as if the wrath of Phil might descend upon us at any moment. As we left the mall, I clutched the bag holding my ugly blouse, privately vowing to wear it the very first time I met Phil Migit.

Finally, the day came when Phil was scheduled to return to town. After spending the day working at the insurance office, I went to work at Waldenbooks in the evening, and Trisha called me there that night.

"Please, you have to stop at the Convent when you are finished working." The Convent was the name we had given the house that Trisha shared with several other young women from our church. Between the Convent and the Bachelors Until Rapture group, I secretly wondered if our church would ever see any weddings. "Phil is going to come to dinner; I'm making steaks on the grill. I need you there, Debbi. Please come." I hesitated. I was scheduled to leave the next day on a vacation to Florida with my friends, Fran, Lora, and Linda. I still had so much packing to finish, but Trisha's pleas swayed me.

"Okay, I'll pop in for just a few minutes. Remember, don't be nervous—just be you." I glanced down at my pink and white striped top, briefly disappointed that I had forgotten to put on the psychedelic shirt I had bought in Phil's honor. I tightened the band on my pigtails. I had been doing inventory at the bookstore and had tied back my long hair to keep it out of the way. Oh well, maybe I would get lucky and Phil would think I was too old to wear pigtails. With that cheerful thought I headed over to the Convent.

The parking lot across from the Convent was full and I recognized a number of cars belonging to others in our group. Obviously, Trisha felt she needed reinforcements. I let myself into the house through the kitchen, stopping to fix a quick soft drink. The sounds of a guitar strumming drew me to the living room, which was filled with my friends and a few new faces. Trisha motioned me over to where she sat on the couch and nodded toward the corner of the room.

"There he is" she whispered reverently. Phil's dark head was bent over the guitar as he strummed the melody of a worship song. Some of the people in the living room were singing softly, while others read their Bibles. I studied him for a few moments, realizing that the picture I had painted in my mind was not quite accurate. I had expected a studious looking, preppy type with short hair and glasses. The only thing that matched that description was the glasses. His worn jeans and brown work boots had seen better days, and he wore a faded flannel shirt with the cuffs rolled up. His hair was dark brown, curling past his shoulders, and I had a suspicion that it might even be longer than mine. He glanced up as he felt me watching him, and I saw that his eyes were dark, also. He looked at me for a moment, a brief smile curling under his mustache, and then he nodded briefly and returned to his playing. I glanced at Trisha.

"He's not what I expected," I accused. Trisha didn't seem to hear me as she sat watching Phil strum the guitar. A moment later the song changed to one I knew well and I soon started to sing along. An hour passed quickly as we were joined by other musicians and singers. Glancing at the clock, I saw it was past eleven, and I still had to pack for my trip. Waving good-bye to my friends, I noticed that Phil glanced up to give a quick nod in my direction. Trisha followed me to my car and when I turned to tell her good-bye, she announced morosely, "He's going to ask you out, you know."

I was stunned. I hadn't seen any indication that Phil was more than remotely aware of my presence that evening. Besides, Trisha had told me she had been up front with Phil about trying to start over in their relationship. Trisha slumped against my Nova.

"I just know he's going to ask me for your phone number."

"Well, first of all, nobody's that big of a jerk! He knows how you feel about him, right?" Trisha nodded. "Yes, but he said he wants to stay 'friends only'." I stepped closer and hugged Trisha as I realized that her big plan had failed.

"Well, I don't want you to give him my number, even if he asks, which he won't," I said. "Plus, I'm leaving town for vacation. A lot can happen in two weeks; just be patient." I hugged Trisha good-bye and headed home to pack. The following morning I left on my trip, secure in the knowledge that by the time I returned, Phil Migit would have moved on.

Chapter Seven

"This is your Phil Migit early warning system. Take cover!" Although Randy was laughing as he ended the phone call, I wasn't. In the months since I had returned home from vacation, Phil had pursued me almost as relentlessly as Jake. Fortunately, Phil often stopped to visit Randy at work before walking down the mall to find me at the bookstore. What he didn't know was that Randy would call me as soon as Phil left and I would find work to do in the backroom, making sure the other employees told him that I shouldn't be disturbed. But I knew I couldn't avoid him forever, and the truth was I didn't want to. Phil had started to attend our singles group on Tuesday evenings at the Convent. He often brought his guitar and led some worship songs before the teaching began, and it wasn't long before the group asked him to start teaching, also. I began to look forward to those meetings, because Phil had a way of explaining scriptures that made them come alive. After the meetings we would all go out to eat, spending hours talking. I noticed that many of my friends had started to ask Phil's advice and counsel as they began to make life decisions. Phil quickly developed a reputation as a man with wisdom, even at the age of twenty-five. The problem was, Trisha still considered him all hers.

Phil had made it a point to explain to me that his feelings for Trisha were for friendship only. But I just couldn't let myself accept his invitations to go out with him. I loved Trisha, and I didn't want to hurt her. I had also explained to Phil that I thought God was directing me to marry a missionary, hoping that Phil would give up and forget about pursuing me. Recently, I had been avoiding the Tuesday meetings completely, which was why Phil was starting to look for me at work.

Now I hurried to the back room of the bookstore and closed the door with a click. Clearing a spot on one of the cluttered work tables, I began the job of sorting the book covers to be returned to the publisher. I imagined that Phil must be asking for me right about now. I knew the store manager, Sandy, could be counted on to send him away.

Finally, I stood and cracked the door open just a bit. Sure enough, I could see Phil standing at the counter, talking to Sandy. I smiled as I saw the heavy suede coat he was wearing, remembering the warmth of that coat when it would settle around my shoulders. One evening after our group had gone bowling, Phil had walked me to my car.

"Aren't you cold?" My friends often teased me about my habit of not wearing a coat, even in the coldest of weather. Since it was November in Illinois, I was a little chilly and the next thing I knew, Phil had wrapped me up in his heavy suede coat. His coat had immediately warmed me, but I had felt something more, as he lifted the collar up to protect me from the wind. I had felt safe and cherished. Since then, Phil often wrapped his coat around me when our group was out together. Now, tears brimmed as I closed the door and returned to my work. Trisha was my friend; I couldn't do this to her.

"He's gone." Sandy opened the door, and I could feel her watching me intently. "Debbi, are you sure you want me to keep sending him away?"

I nodded without turning, and after a moment Sandy left, closing the door behind her. The book covers blurred before my eyes as tears began to fall. I lay my head on the table as the truth seemed to take my breath way. *I was in love with Phil Migit! Great. How had that happened?* I was overcome with conflicting emotions: joy, excitement, and hopelessness. *Now what?*

"Let's elope."

I ignored the suggestion and continued to look at the latest issue of Bride's magazine. We only had three months to plan this wedding, and I didn't have time for jokes. There were invitations to choose, a dress to buy, a reception to plan, Trisha to tell—

A few days after my revelation about my feelings for Phil, I had agreed to meet with him after work. That night Phil calmly told me that he loved me, but would not allow himself to fall in love with me.

"If God is really telling you to marry a missionary, then I am in danger of coveting another man's wife," he explained. "You need to ask God what His plan is for your life. Unless He tells you it includes me, I will be leaving the area." My heart broke at the thought of never seeing him again, and I spent days in prayer, asking for confirmation that we could pursue our relationship. When that assurance came, Phil and I approached Trisha and explained what was happening between us. Trisha accepted our announcement with grace and agreed to see where the relationship took us. But I don't think anyone imagined it would take us down the aisle quite so quickly. We had only dated for three weeks before we knew we wanted to spend the rest of our lives together.

Our next step was to try and discern if what we felt was genuinely given by God and if it was His plan for us to be married. I told Phil that I didn't want to talk about marriage until we had clear direction from God, since we might get caught up in the idea of a wedding before we had God's blessing for our marriage. We spent a week-end traveling to Ohio to visit Phil's parents and his two sisters, Val and Kim. Later Phil introduced me to his brother, Glen, and his family, and I took Phil to dinner at my parent's home. We realized they were all waiting to hear what our plans were, and so were we. Phil was twenty-five and I was twenty-two; we were anxious to get on with our lives together, if that was really what God had planned for us.

One evening as I traveled from my insurance job to the

bookstore to work the late shift, I sensed the Lord speak to my heart.

"Phil will ask you to marry him tonight. You can say 'Yes'." My heart skipped a beat and I couldn't wait to see Phil. I arrived at the mall a few minutes early and raced to the jewelry store across the hall from Waldenbooks. I had resisted looking at engagement rings, but now I took a brochure and put it into my purse. Then I hurried to the bookstore, eager for him to meet me after work.

Leaving the store that evening, I slipped the folded brochure into the pocket of Phil's suede coat. His attention was on me, however, and I realized he wasn't aware of what the brochure advertised. Later, as we drove to our favorite restaurant, Phil looked at me.

"I have something to tell you. I spent the evening praying about our relationship, and I believe God spoke clearly to me tonight." He was so solemn that I felt my pulse quicken. *What if I had heard wrong and Phil said that God had told him that we were not to be married. What if he was going to say good-bye?*

"Will you marry me?" I gave him a soft smile.

"Look in your coat pocket," I said. Phil held the wheel with one hand as he pulled the jewelry brochure from his pocket. He glanced down and then back at me and I said, "I heard from God tonight, too. Yes, I will marry you."

Phil and I were married on a beautiful spring day in

April, 1978. As we stood in the receiving line, I saw Trisha and Randy approach, and I gripped my husband's hand tighter.

"It was a beautiful wedding," Trisha said as she leaned in to kiss my cheek. I studied her closely for a moment, relieved at the sincerity of her happiness for us. It seemed that Phil and I were destined to start our new life together with no shadows from the past.

A few weeks later, I eagerly thumbed through the proofs of our wedding pictures, smiling at the photo of Phil and me standing with our parents on the steps of the church. But, as I continued to scan the pictures, I caught a glimpse of a man in the background; he seemed to have turned his head just as the picture was snapped. At that moment, I realized that our wedding day had included one uninvited guest: Jake.

Chapter Eight

CHRISTMAS EVE, 1978

It was our first Christmas together, and I was excited as Phil and I packed our VW bug with gifts and food. As an added bonus, snow had started to fall early in the afternoon, and it looked like we were destined for a white Christmas. We only had ten miles to travel to my parent's home, but I was eager to get on the road before the streets became too slick. My twin brother Dave, and his wife Kathy, were visiting from Minnesota, and my cousin Brenda had driven up from Missouri. My younger brother, Scott, was only eleven, so at least someone would be receiving toys the next morning. It was going to be a wonderful Christmas.

"Could you stop by the post office on the way out of town?" I tried to balance the tray of cookies on my lap as Phil spun the car through the snow. He obligingly parked in front of the small brick building that housed the local post office, and a moment later he was back, carrying several Christmas cards and a small box that held a fruit cake from Phil's Aunt Dickie. I quickly began to open the cards, secretly thrilling to read the address: Mr. and Mrs. Phil Migit. At the bottom of the pile was a white envelope, and as I glanced at the address I felt a chill that had nothing to do with the weather. I knew that handwriting. Glancing at Phil, I was relieved that he seemed pre-occupied with his driving, and I slowly tore open the envelope. A red faced Santa Claus peered up at me. I flipped open the card and read:

> Dear Deborah,
> Well, it's lasted longer than I thought—I only gave your marriage six months. I wanted to let you know that I will always be waiting for you. You need to realize that you will probably never have anyone's baby but mine. But if you do happen to get pregnant, make sure and name it after me—since I will eventually be the father anyway.
>
> I'm waiting.
> Jake

My hands shook as I jammed the card back in the envelope.

"What's that?" Phil glanced at me and I gave him a bright smile.

"Nothing," I said, and quickly changed the subject to what my mom had planned for Christmas dinner. It was usually pretty easy to distract Phil with the promise of ham. But, inside I was sick to think that the memory of Jake might mar my first Christmas with my new husband.

Hours later I sat cuddled with Phil in front of my parent's fireplace. The room was fragrant with spices as we sipped our mulled cider and watched the flickering flames. The snow had continued to fall and we decided to spend the night. My bother, Scott, had gone to bed a few moments earlier, hoping that sleep would make Christmas morning come more quickly. Suddenly, the peace was shattered by a loud crash. For a moment we all stared at each other, trying to decide what had caused the noise.

"Sounds like someone's window was broken." Phil switched on the porch light and peered out side. A moment later he turned and said with regret, "Well, Merry Christmas to us." Pointing to where we had parked our red VW bug, Phil indicated the shattered window. A large rock lay in the snow beside the car.

"Now, who would do such a thing?" my mom asked, as Phil and Dave hurried out to cover the broken window with a plastic tarp. I said nothing, but I knew. Settling down to sleep that night, I thought about the first night when Jake had shown up unannounced, and I had finally let him into the house, and my life. I knew that God had told me to stay away from him, and I continued to pay the price for my disobedience. I just didn't realize, at that time, how steep the price would be.

The following spring, we decided to buy the auto body business from Phil's employer. Although we both dreamed of full-time ministry someday, we knew that God was saying, "*Wait.*" In the meantime, we needed to make some decisions about our future. Phil often said he crashed into the auto body business by accident. One snowy day as he returned home from college, Phil hit a patch of ice and landed in a ditch. Riding home in the wrecker, he convinced the body shop owner to hire him part time to help pay for the repairs on his car. At the end of the semester, Phil had made the decision to leave college and the teaching degree he had been pursuing. He had discovered he had a gift for auto body repair and painting, and he had been in the trade ever since. He was now the shop foreman, overseeing three other workers.

While praying and reading my Bible one day, I happened across a scripture that said, "Prepare your outside work, make it fit for yourself in the field, and afterwards build your house" (Proverbs 24:27, NKJV). I sensed the Lord stirring the thought inside me that we were going to start our own business. Later that night I shared my impressions with Phil.

"Actually, I have been thinking and praying about starting my own business," Phil responded. "Let's pray about it together and see what God has in mind." Still, we were both amazed when a few days later, his employer casually offered to sell the business to us; within two weeks we were officially business owners. Soon after that, I began teaching at the Christian school that was operated by our local church, where Phil and I were also the youth leaders. We were busy and happy, but something was beginning to concern me.

I had always assumed children were part of my future. When my twin brother, Dave, and I were eleven, our brother Scott was born, and I immediately knew children would be part of my destiny. I liked nothing better than rocking my baby brother to sleep, singing him the lullabies my mother had sung to me. I quickly became an expert at feeding, soothing, and even diaper changes. There was nothing more satisfying to me than to cuddle an infant or child in my arms. By the time I reached high school age, I was babysitting every week-end in our suburban neighborhood. I even chose to enter a child care class in high school and worked at a pre-school during part of my school day. At church I was known as the Pied Piper, because there always seemed to be a trail of children following me. It had never occurred to me that I would not be able to bear children; surely God wouldn't give me such a strong desire if that wasn't His plan for me.

Early in our marriage we had decided to let God determine when our children would come. But, it had been three years and Phil and I were beginning to face the truth. We were infertile. I preferred that term to the other one: barren. There was such harshness to that word, as if God had deemed me unfit in some way to raise a child. My image of myself as loved and cherished by God was being shaken to the core. My relationship with Him began to revolve around that one question: *Why?*

CHRISTMAS 1981

It was our third Christmas together, and I suspected that I was pregnant. I couldn't wait until the day after Christmas when I could go to the doctor to confirm it. Until then I was keeping my secret. The past few years had been like a roller coaster ride as we waited every month to see if I was pregnant. Now I wanted to spare Phil any disappointment if this was another false hope.

On Christmas night Phil and I drove to my grandmother's house to deliver her Christmas gift. Grandma Flynn's small apartment was filled with family who had gathered for the day. My mother's Irish family was large, with eight children and many, many grandchildren. My grandmother was famous for her homemade pies, and within minutes Phil was happily savoring his favorite: coconut cream. I had settled into a corner of the kitchen to catch up with my cousin, Krista, when another cousin walked through the door.

Adam was actually my double cousin. His mother, Bonnie, was my mom's sister and his dad, Chuck, was my dad's brother. I had been concerned about Adam lately. I knew he had been drinking and probably abusing drugs, too. Frankly, I was surprised to see him at the party. It took less than a minute for me to realize that Adam was high.

And for some reason, I was going to be the target of his anger and pain.

"Well, if it isn't my sweet cousin, Debbi." Adam approached me as I went to find my coat. My alarms had started going off the minute he entered the room and I knew Phil and I needed to leave. Although I had never had a cross word with Adam, I knew in my spirit that he hated me, and I needed to get out of his way. But the rooms were too crowded, and Adam quickly cornered me in my grandmother's bedroom.

"You know, I hate you, don't you?" I looked into Adam's eyes and shivered. What I saw wasn't Adam at all, and fear began to pound through me. "You always thought you were better than me, and I know you were the one who called the police on me last summer when I was drinking at the park. I got arrested, you know, and it was all your fault!"

"That's not true, Adam," I said quietly, trying to back away. "Someone else must have reported you; I promise it wasn't me." Tears filled my eyes as I remembered all the years my parents had picked up Adam and his brothers, taking them to Sunday School with us. Adam's parents had divorced years ago, and their family had never recovered.

"You know I love you. And Jesus loves you, too." My words had the effect of throwing gasoline on a fire. In years past, Adam had a relationship with Jesus, and I had continued to pray for him to return to his first love. Now I saw none of the Adam I used to know and love. This was a stranger, and as the hate flared in his eyes, I knew he intended to kill me. I tried to move away, but he grabbed me by the throat and began to choke me. His thumbs pressed on my windpipe, and I began to see spots in front of my eyes. In my haze I could hear Adam screaming about how much he hated me and wanted me dead. I began to think he would get his wish when, suddenly, I was free. I stood gasping for air as Phil and Dave hauled Adam out of the room. Others gathered around me as I sat down abruptly on Grandma's chenille-covered bed. There had never been any arguments or violence at our family gatherings, and everyone was in shock about what had just happened.

Phil came and sat beside me. "Are you ok?" He lightly touched my throat and I leaned on his shoulder.

"Please," I whispered. "Just take me home." My parents hadn't arrived at the party yet, and I asked those in the room with us to keep quiet about what had happened. I knew it would hurt them deeply. One of my uncles had taken Adam home to sleep it off, and Phil had grimly told him that if he ever approached me again, we would call the police. Phil quickly bundled me into my coat, and we made the trip home. As I entered our apartment, I shivered again at the memory of Adam's eyes, and the hatred I had seen there. I realized that it hadn't been my cousin I faced tonight, but whatever demons he had allowed into his life. But the emotional hurt was even stronger than the pain in my throat, and I cried myself to sleep.

The pain woke me at about two a.m. Something was

seriously wrong with me, and after a moment I knew. I had lost our baby.

Chapter Nine

SUMMER 1985

"Debbi, do you want to go to see Bobby Connor with us tonight?" My friend Nancy called me one morning with the invitation. Nancy and her sister Alice were married to brothers, and they both pastored Vineyard churches. Now that Phil and I were attending the Vineyard, we had many opportunities to see speakers like John Wimber, Mike Bickle, Randy Clark, and many others. I loved the conferences, especially the worship and the prophetic ministry. I had never seen Bobby Connor in person, but had heard exciting reports about his ministry, so I didn't hesitate to say yes. Maybe he would have some word of encouragement for me about a baby. It had been four years since the miscarriage. Phil and I had started to see a fertility specialist, Dr. Shay. Many tests and procedures had revealed one thing—there was no specific problem—we were just infertile. I had started to feel like my whole existence was defined by that one word.

That evening, Nancy and I joined Alice in the ballroom of the hotel that was hosting the conference. Alice was especially eager for ministry because she and her husband,

George, were planning to move to England soon to join a missions team. Bobby Connor was fascinating to hear, and before I knew it, Nancy, Alice, and I were standing in line, waiting for personal ministry. Then, suddenly, it was my turn.

"What is on your heart tonight?" Bobby Connor had a gentle manner, and I was quickly put at ease.

"I would like a baby," I said simply. Bobby nodded, and then closed his eyes to pray. A second later Bobby jumped back with a startled exclamation and I looked up to see him watching me in surprise.

"I felt life," Bobby said in awe. "I literally felt a baby kicking me from the inside of my stomach. I've never experienced that before! There is life in you already. Understand, I don't know exactly what this means, or how it will manifest, but God has heard your cry and you will have a child. In the Spirit, you are already pregnant." I floated home that night, eagerly planning my next few months. We were going to have a baby! What I didn't realize was that I had much to learn about the ways God speaks to us, and my lessons were about to begin.

Christmas 1985

The beeping of the cash register told me that Jim was ringing up more sales. The bookstore had been busy lately as the holidays neared, and I welcomed the extra work that kept my mind occupied. Glancing up at the open doorway that led out to the main entrance of the mall, I stepped back behind a bookcase to continue my work. For some reason I had started to feel exposed as I stood working near the front of the store. The feeling had been plaguing me for a couple of weeks and I didn't know why. I did however, know who.

It was odd that I had been thinking about Jake so much lately. It had been almost eight years since I had heard from him. After the events of our first Christmas Eve, Phil had tried to get me to reveal Jake's address, but I refused. I couldn't think of any positive outcome if Phil and Jake met face to face. When it seemed that Jake was going to leave us alone, Phil and I had settled into our marriage, and over time we forgot about Jake.

But now the uneasy feeling was back, and I scanned the hallway once more, then turned to gather up a stack of books to be shelved. The afternoon passed quickly as I rang up gift cards and helped last minute shoppers with their Christmas lists.

"Thank you, enjoy your holidays!" I smiled and handed a bag to the elderly gentleman who had purchased a cookbook for his wife. The crowds had started to clear out as dinner time approached, and I signaled to Jim that I was going to take a break. I headed to the back room, eager for five minutes off my feet.

"Deborah." Jake stood in front of me, blocking the aisle that lead to the back room, and relative safety. "How are you?" Jake leaned casually against the bookshelf, but I knew from experience there was nothing casual about his intent. The uneasiness I had felt for the past few weeks had warned me of this meeting, but I still wasn't prepared.

"I'm fine." I gave Jake a quick smile and tried to brush past him, but he stood firm. Business-like, I asked, "Is there a book you need? I am going on my break, but I'm sure Jim would be happy to help you."

"I'm here for you," Jake responded quietly.

I tried to study his face, but Jake was wearing his sunglasses, even in the store, and it was hard to determine his mood. Jake had often left his glasses on for that reason, and it always disconcerted me.

I came right to the point. "What do you want, Jake?"

"You know what I want," he said. Behind Jake I could see Jim watching us and I gave a quick nod to indicate that I was okay. Jim busied himself in the next aisle, and I tried to reassure myself that Jake couldn't do anything to me here in the middle of the store.

"So you're still married?" His question was almost an accusation.

"Happily," I replied.

"But no children." Jake had finally removed his sunglasses and I was shocked by the simmering anger I saw there.

"Not yet," I said brightly. "But we enjoy trying."

Anger flared, and Jake leaned in closer. "There won't be any children with him, Deborah. I told you, you won't ever have anyone's baby but mine. Think about that." A moment later Jake was gone, leaving me shaking.

"Are you ok?" Jim came up and touched my arm. "What a creep! I heard what he said. Who was he?"

"A mistake," I whispered. "A big mistake."

SUMMER 1986

Glancing around the crowded sanctuary, I sensed the excitement in the air. Trinity Church was hosting a conference featuring Gary Weins, and our worship team had been asked to provide a set for the evening service. Phil had been leading worship at the Vineyard for several years now, but this was the largest crowd we had ever stood before. I was a little nervous, but the strong sense of anointing was quickly canceling my fear. I sensed this would be a night to remember.

Two hours later I was still shaking from the impact of Gary's words. He had shared story after story of God's amazing miracles of healing, and my faith had never been higher. So, when Gary announced at the end of the service that he felt a leading to pray for barren couples, my heart leaped. Phil squeezed my hand, and together we walked to the front of the church to receive prayer. This was certainly not the first time Phil and I had stood together like this, asking God to bless us with children. But as Gary approached us, I knew that God was about to give us a special message tonight.

"Your children will come, but not in the way you expect." I opened my eyes and saw Gary facing us as he delivered those simple words. Then he moved on. My mind and heart battled as I tried to discern the meaning of his words. What I heard was "Yes—and no." *What did that mean?* I closed my eyes again, and a moment later I was aware of the beautiful scent of roses. Glancing behind to see who had approached us, I realized that Phil and I were the only ones left standing at the altar; no one else was near. A moment later the scent faded, but I knew I would never forget that fragrance.

SIX MONTHS LATER …

"The treatment is called Clomid and it should help regulate your hormones and make it possible for you to conceive." Dr. Shay scribbled a note on the prescription pad, and then handed it to me. He had kept his tone hopeful, but I knew that my doctor was becoming discouraged, too. Dr. Shay was a fertility specialist, and I began to feel guilty for ruining his stats. He had been working with Phil and me for seven years, and he seemed genuinely puzzled by our inability to conceive. We had tried so many tests, treatments, and even a few surgeries, but nothing helped. According to Dr. Shay, there was really no discernable reason for us to be infertile. We just were.

"Debbi, there is another possibility." My pulse quickened. Although I regularly studied fertility books and medical journals, maybe there was something new I hadn't heard of yet.

"In vitro." Dr. Shay offered his solution.

I shook my head. "We've talked about that, but it's just too expensive. Our insurance won't cover it, and we can't afford it."

"Well, I think maybe you can." Dr. Shay smiled for the first time since I had entered the room and said, "I want to make a special offer to you and Phil. I will do the procedure as many times as necessary for a very nominal fee." The price he named was so low that it took my breath away.

"Are you sure?" I asked, as hope made my heart leap.

"Debbi, if there was ever a couple that deserved to have children, it is you and Phil. I want to make this available to you. Go home and talk to Phil. The offer is open whenever you decide you are ready."

I felt as if I was floating, rather than driving home. Laughing out loud I began to thank God for providing this opportunity after so many years of disappointment.

I decided to head straight to the auto body shop to share the news with Phil, but as I turned off the highway I heard God's unmistakable voice.

"*No.*"

I shook my head to clear it and tried to concentrate on the miracle that was about to occur. We were finally going to have a baby. We had no problem with the idea of in vitro fertilization, but as I had shared with Dr. Shay, the price had made it impossible for us. But, no longer…

"*This is not my plan for you.*" Again the voice intruded on my celebration. Tears began to form in my eyes even as I tried to navigate the back roads to our business.

"Please, God," I whispered. "Please." The tears fell freely and I finally had to stop the car or risk an accident.

"Why?"

God answered my question with one of His own. "*Debbi, at the end of your days, would you rather say, 'I had ten children' or 'I obeyed God'?*"

I hoped I didn't offend God by taking so long to reply.

"I will obey you," I said. Even as I spoke the words, grief warred with peace. For a moment I felt a physical ache so strong I groaned in pain. Oh, how I longed for our baby. But even more, I longed to please God. In the end, there was only one choice. A long time ago I had made a decision to live my life by hearing and obeying God; no matter what He asked from me. For a moment I thought of Abraham as he prepared to sacrifice Isaac, and I had just a glimpse of what it must have cost him. But even as I remembered that story, I also remembered the answer God had provided to Abraham. I started the car again and drove home, filled with hope, even as the tears dried on my cheeks.

Chapter Ten

CHRISTMAS EVE 1986

I was pregnant. Wrapping my arms around my tummy, I hugged the sweet knowledge to myself. I imagined I could even feel a fluttering inside already, although I knew that was impossible. It was too soon, of course. I squirmed in my seat like a ten-year-old about to enter Disneyland. The woman sitting on the opposite side of the waiting room darted a glance up from her magazine, and I willed myself to be composed. She looked about twenty-five-years-old, and she was very pregnant. For a moment I felt a familiar twinge of jealousy, but quickly pushed it away. The old patterns would need to change. If I was truly pregnant, I would finally be able to look at other mommies-to-be and feel a sense of kinship instead of sadness or anger. Joy simmered, and I gave the woman a companionable smile. Casually crossing my legs, I smoothed my navy slacks, brushing off a spot of salt that lingered from my walk through the slush outside. My navy shoes were soaked, a testament to my reluctance to wear boots. Although I had lived in Illinois all of my life, I had a stubborn resistance to wearing winter clothing. It had been snowing for hours, and the road crews were working overtime to make sure everyone could make it home for the holidays. Another wave of excitement shivered through me. *Pregnant, and on Christmas Eve, no less! It's perfect.* My lips curved in an irrepressible grin. The memories of eight years of trying to conceive, several surgeries, and months of fertility drugs faded away in the miracle of the moment. None of it mattered now. All that was important was that tonight I would be giving my husband the gift of a lifetime.

On the floor next to me, a little girl rummaged through the meager contents of a toy box. Blocks quickly littered the floor as she dug deep for her prize. I smiled as I watched the little girl pull out a stuffed green frog and give it a hug. *What was the frog's name?* I realized that I would soon be very familiar with the dinosaur and many other characters. I was a traditionalist, visions of a nursery inhabited by Pooh and his friends teased my mind.

It was 2:00 p.m. and Dr. Shay's office was nearly empty. On the other side of the reception desk I could see the nurses, Janet and Chris, as they took a moment from their work to sample the apple cake that a patient had brought in to the office. They had offered me a piece earlier, but I was too excited to eat, although the spicy aroma that still lingered from the cake was a nice treat. The window around the desk was decorated, and Christmas lights blinked, causing the silver garland to sparkle. I couldn't imagine a better setting to finally receive the positive news of my pregnancy.

Down the hall a door opened, then closed, and I heard Dr. Shay's voice as he spoke to Janet. After eight years of battling infertility, Dr. Shay, Janet, and Chris had become almost like family in my mind. When Dr. Shay had examined me a few moments ago, it seemed he was as excited as I was when he announced, "It looks like the Clomid finally did the trick!" What he didn't say was, "It's a good thing, too." I knew that if I hadn't become pregnant this time, we would have to try another method. Because of the long term side effects, six months of Clomid was all I was allowed. Phil had been a little wary of the Clomid from the beginning. The stories of multiple births worried him, although I explained that other drugs were more likely to bring that result. "Did you remind the doctor that you are a twin, and that twins run in your family?" Phil had cautioned. "Tell him we want a baby, not a litter!" We had both laughed, but I knew that Phil was still uncertain about having one baby, let alone two. Since my grandmother was a twin, and two of her eight children had produced twins, I could understand Phil's caution. I had dreamed of having several children and now, at age thirty-one, time was getting short. Caught up in the magic of the moment, I allowed myself a brief hope that I really might be carrying twins.

Dr. Shay's voice was muffled as he moved down the hall. I nervously picked up a magazine and tried to distract myself. Janet had taken my blood test and asked me to stay in the waiting room for a few minutes while they confirmed my pregnancy. A toothless baby grinned up at me from the cover of a magazine. When I had first come to see Dr. Shay, I poured over the parenting magazines in his waiting room, soaking up every bit of wit and wisdom they offered. After the first year, though, I'd studiously begun to avoid them, in favor of more generic reading material. Today I quickly thumbed through the pages, hoping to catch up. There was so much to learn.

"Debbi?" Janet leaned around the door frame. "Dr. Shay can see you now." I carefully replaced the magazine and followed Janet to the private office Phil and I had visited once, so many years ago. I tried to picture how Dr. Shay would officially announce my pregnancy. One time, about four years ago, I had been waiting in an exam room when I heard Dr. Shay enter the room next door. His booming voice came through as he announced to the patient, "Congratulations lady. You are pregnant!" Tears suddenly clogged my throat at that memory, and the years of longing to hear those words.

For eight years, Phil and I had faced the pain of infertility, and my faith had been shaken to its foundation. But now, finally, I would have the desire of my heart. Just a few minutes more—

Juggling my purse and packages, I tried to stay upright on the slick front porch. The snow was coming down even harder now and the cold, wet stuff was oozing into my good navy shoes. I worked the key into the lock and pushed open the front door of the duplex. Purse and packages landed with a thump in the entryway as I stumbled into the apartment and closed out the cold. Slipping my shoes off, I watched the ice make a puddle on the tile floor. A little stream meandered toward a pile of letters and cards that had fallen through the mail slot. The red and green envelopes proclaimed Christmas cards, and I just couldn't face those right now. So many would be accompanied by pictures of children; nieces, nephews, friends. I would read them later, much later.

Walking into the bedroom, I heard Dr. Shay's words echo in my mind. "I'm sorry, Debbi, the blood test was negative." I mechanically changed into jeans and a tee shirt, noticing the black velvet outfit I had laid out this morning, in anticipation of a celebration tonight. I quickly shoved it into the back of the closet, thankful that Phil hadn't seen it. He would wonder what the occasion was. I had carefully guarded my "secret" for the past two weeks, and hadn't told Phil about my appointment today. We'd had so many disappointments I hadn't wanted to get his hopes up—just mine. Now we would have a quiet Christmas Eve without Phil having to know about my latest heartbreak. I would have to tell him eventually. Dr. Shay had explained that the Clomid treatment was finished, and we would need to discuss other options.

But not tonight; this was Christmas Eve, and I was determined that Phil would be spared the disappointment that I had endured today. I would make a nice dinner and give him the hand carved chess set I had seen him admiring in the mall. A small sob caught in my throat as I thought of the other gift I had planned to present to Phil tonight; the promise of our baby. What a Christmas it would have been.

Just last week, we had allowed ourselves to dream a little about what the holidays would be like with a child. "You know, we don't have to put up a tree just for the two of us," Phil had said. We had just finished snapping the tree together and were trying to wrestle it into the corner. I had to admit that the artificial tree looked a little forlorn. I quickly dug through the box of ornaments and handed Phil the Snoopy and Woodstock ornaments that I had purchased the first year we had been married. My employee discount had helped start our ornament collection. Our tree looked like a tribute to Charles Schultz.

"We need a tree," I stubbornly insisted. "We are a family, even if it's just the two of us. Besides, where else will you put all the gifts you are going to buy me?"

Phil smirked at that, and then said, "Did I ever tell you about staying up all night one Christmas Eve, putting together Barbie's dream house for my sister?"

"Well, it couldn't have been any worse that putting together my brother's grocery store," I countered. "We had to glue labels on every single can of vegetables, and the cardboard store kept collapsing." I handed Phil the star and watched as he placed it on the top of the tree.

As the lights twinkled around us, we held each other as Phil whispered, "Don't worry, we'll be building dream houses and grocery stores again some day, I promise."

Now I shook off the sadness that threatened to overwhelm me as I began to prepare our traditional Christmas Eve dinner of roasted lamb.

Moments later, I heard Phil's key in the front door. I worked up my most festive smile and hurried to the living room.

"Hi honey, I'm home." Phil grinned and enveloped me in his arms.

"Merry Christmas." I kissed him, and then busied myself with picking up the Christmas cards that were still lying on the floor. "Did you have a good day?"

"Sure. The crew worked until about noon, and then I treated them all to pizza. I would have been home sooner, but I had some last minute shopping to do. How was your day?" It was quiet for a moment and I realized Phil was watching me carefully.

I shrugged nonchalantly. "Oh, the usual. The bookstore was full of men who were doing their Christmas shopping at the last minute." I gave Phil a genuine smile. In the eight years that we had been married, I had never been able to convince Phil to shop before Christmas Eve. He claimed it was his own special tradition. Phil walked into the living room and said, "I was surprised that you don't have the tree lit. Since you are the "Spirit of Christmas Present," I figured you would have turned it on as soon as you came home. Is anything wrong? " Phil flipped the switch and the tree sparkled with colorful lights and Peanuts characters.

"Oh, I guess I was so focused on making dinner I didn't think about it." I could tell that Phil wasn't convinced, so I quickly led him into the kitchen where the aroma of lamb was certain to distract him. Probing questions gave way to making gravy, and I was able to push my grief aside for a while longer.

It was almost midnight when I slipped into the living room and switched the tree lights on again. Phil and I had exchanged our gifts after dinner, and I glanced down at my beautiful new watch. For a last minute shopper, he did all right, I acknowledged. I curled up in the recliner and retrieved the mail I had placed on the table earlier in the evening. There were so many Christmas cards. Sadness threatened to overwhelm me again, as I remembered just the other day, when I had practiced writing "Phil, Debbi, and Kate Migit," in preparation for next year's Christmas cards. Kate. That is what I wanted to name our first daughter.

"God, I don't understand," I whispered. "Why is it that so many people can have babies easily, often when they don't even want them? But Phil and I can't. Have we done something wrong? Do you think we will be bad parents?" My tears splashed down on the brightly colored envelopes. With a sigh, I picked them up and looked at the return addresses: Phil's sister, Val, in Oklahoma; my twin brother, Dave, who lived in Minnesota. Those cards definitely contained children's pictures. I laid them aside for the moment and picked up a red envelope from the bottom of the pile: Vickie Harper from Bee Branch, Arkansas. *Who on earth?* I checked the mailing address again and saw that it was indeed meant for me. Happy for a moment's distraction, I carefully tore open the envelope and pulled out a Christmas card. A letter and picture fluttered to the floor, and my breath caught as I picked up the picture and saw a beautiful little girl, about three- years-old. Apparently there was no avoiding children's pictures tonight. I quickly unfolded the handwritten letter and began to read.

Dear Debbi,

I don't know if you remember me. It has taken me such a long time to find you. I know it has been almost twenty years since we've seen each other, but I hope you've thought of me, as I've thought of you. We were just thir-teen-years-old when I last saw you, remember? My dad had accepted the pastorate at a church in Arkansas and we had to move away. I don't know why, but I have really felt like I needed to contact you this Christmas and tell you what has been going on in my life. I've been married for a number of years now. My husband and I wanted to have children right away, but that wasn't to be. I don't know if you can understand the pain of wanting children more than anything, and still not being able to conceive. It tested our faith and trust in God to the limits. But as you can see from the enclosed picture, God is faithful! This is our daughter, Angela. We adopted her this year, and she is the love of our lives! I can't tell you the joy this little girl has brought to us. I just felt like I had to share our story with you this Christmas. I pray that all is well with you and you are being blessed by God.

Love,
Vickie

I stared at the letter and picture as the tears fell. I hadn't heard from Vickie in almost twenty years. And then tonight, of all nights, I had received such a letter! I held my breath as I sensed God's presence all around me. *Adoption, was that what God had in mind for us?* Early in our marriage, Phil and I had talked about adopting a child some day. But we had been so caught up in the fertility treatments that the thought had been pushed aside. I let the idea begin to form in my mind, but I quickly stopped.

There was one question, and I whispered it in my prayer, "God, could I love an adopted child as I would a biological child?" The answer was immediate and certain.

"*I adopted you. Do you doubt My love for you?*"

"Never, Lord!" Even as I had questioned God's reasons for withholding what we desired so much, I had never doubted His love.

Adoption. Now the word took on a whole new meaning. My mind was filled with adoption stories from the Bible: Moses, and yes, even Jesus. I suddenly remembered a Christmas, so many years ago, when I had been eleven-years-old. My family had returned from the Christmas program at church that night, and the phone was ringing as we walked in the door. I had watched as my mother listened to the wonderful news—their closest friends Marlene and Carroll had received a call that day from an adoption agency. They had a new daughter, and they had named her Joy. I always remembered that as one the happiest Christmas's I had ever known. Now I wondered if God had planted a seed in my heart that was just now ready to blossom. In just a moment, it seemed that my whole focus changed. Gone was the sharp grief of infertility, although I knew that it would take time to complete the healing. In its place was something I hadn't expected to feel again for a long time.

Hope.

Chapter Eleven

"I had the dream again." Phil and I sat drinking coffee at the kitchen table. Several weeks had passed since that amazing Christmas Eve, and we had spent the time exploring our feelings concerning adoption.

"The baby dream?" Phil asked quietly.

"Yes, but there was more detail this time. I was standing outside, looking up at the sky. There were clouds everywhere and suddenly a baby boy was floating down right toward me." Watching Phil carefully, I added, "But this time I saw him clearly. He was so beautiful, with dark, curly hair and—"

"And?" Phil prompted.

"He was African American."

Phil studied me for a moment and then said simply, "Okay."

"Okay?" I repeated, in surprise. "We've never even discussed the possibility of adopting a baby of another race. There could be a lot of challenges we haven't thought of. Are you sure?"

"Well, the way I see it, if this baby that keeps floating around in your dreams is really given to us by God, then I believe God will give us what we need to raise him. There are challenges in parenting, whether you have children by birth or adoption. I'm not naïve about some of the added demands of transracial adoption, but God must have a reason to put this particular child with us. I say we trust Him." Phil smiled and hugged me.

"Oh, by the way," Phil added with a grin as he walked out the back door. "Boys aren't beautiful."

Smiling back I stated with confidence, "Just wait till you see this one."

As soon as Phil left for work I took out my adoption folder and notebook. Although we were sure that adoption was the direction God was leading us, we also agreed that we wished He had been a little more specific on Christmas Eve. The name and phone number of an adoption agency would have been a great help! But lacking that, I had started to amass quite a file of information on adoption agencies from all over the country and even a few from other countries. Now that we had another piece of the puzzle, I was anxious to begin narrowing our search. The remainder of my morning was spent calling agencies that offered transracial adoptions.

That evening over dinner, I shared some new information with Phil. "It's called Catholic Social Services, right here in town," I told him excitedly as I passed the lasagna. "They place African American and Caucasian newborns. According to the information I was given on the phone, it looks like we qualify in terms of age and income and—" My voice trailed off as I noticed Phil's questioning look.

"And we are not Catholic," he said. "Isn't that one of the qualifications?" I shook my head.

"No, not at all. I mean, they do give preference to Catholic families I suppose, and we would be charged a fee, rather than the donation requested from a Catholic couple. But," I hurried on, "we knew already that there would be costs involved, right?"

"How much?" Phil took a bite of his bread and waited for the verdict.

"Um, about seven thousand dollars, give or take," I answered.

"We give, they take, right?" Phil stopped eating and set aside the rest of his meal. That was not a good sign; he loved my lasagna. "Did you tell them we don't own our home yet, that we still rent?" Phil asked.

"They said that is fine," I answered with a bright smile. "It's better of course to have a house, but as long as the caseworker is satisfied that our home is clean and the baby has his own room, that shouldn't be a problem." I tried to bring the focus back to the positive, but Phil's quick mind continued with questions.

"What about lawyer fees? Are those included?"

"No," I said quietly, recognizing the warning signs. The cost was Phil's responsibility and he didn't take on debt easily. "The legal fees could be between eight hundred to twelve hundred dollars, depending on what is involved in court fees." The silence was broken after a moment.

"Not yet." Phil shook his head and stood. "I can't feel good about borrowing that much money when we don't even have our own home yet. The business needs more time to get established. We need to save for a house first and then we can look into the adoption. It's too soon."

Too soon? A few moments later I clicked the dishwasher door shut a little more firmly than it needed. *How could it be too soon?* I scrubbed the counter until it gleamed and then continued rubbing. We had been married for eight years. *Yes, all of our money had gone back into our business, but that was a good thing, right?* The bank was always happy with our profit reports every year. Our credit was great. Surely the bank would loan us the money for the adoption now, and later a house, too. I looked around the duplex. The rooms were large and cheery; there was no reason for a caseworker to have any questions about our home environment. But inside I knew Phil was right. In our experience, God seemed to be very firm about doing things in a certain order. I was reminded of the way God had directed us to buy the auto body business. We had been told to establish our business first, and then buy our home. That had been seven years ago, and although our investment was growing, it still took all of our resources and left little for savings.

It was time to ask God some serious questions. I gathered up my Bible and notebook and went to the patio to pray. I could hear the television in the living room and knew Phil was giving me space to work out my emotions. I settled into the deck chair and opened my Bible. I often loved to start in Psalms, but tonight I opened my Bible to read, "Enlarge the place of your tent; and let them stretch out the curtains of your dwellings; Do not spare, lengthen your cords; and strengthen your stakes" (Isaiah 54:2, NKJV). My hands trembled as I re-read the passage. "Enlarge the place of your tent—" Could it be that God was telling us it was time to buy a home? What were the odds of reading such a passage just moments after our conversation? I glanced towards the kitchen door and thought of showing the passage to Phil, but that didn't seem to be the answer. I knew Phil was overwhelmed with running the business and contemplating the adoption. This wasn't a matter to share; it was a matter for prayer. I smiled at my unintended rhyme. Then I began to pray.

Chapter Twelve

FEBRUARY 14, 1987

The scent of roses filled my small office, and I took a moment from my work to admire them. The delicate pink buds were mixed with tiny white baby's breath and a lacy Valentine card. The arrangement had been waiting for me when I returned from lunch, and I couldn't wait to tell Phil how beautiful they were. I turned back to my desk, but continued to sneak a peek as I worked. I had changed jobs soon after Christmas, and I was enjoying the solitude of having my own office at the insurance company where I now worked. I often felt guilty about how quickly I finished my work, but my boss had assured me that once my paperwork was done, all I needed to do was answer the telephone for the rest of the afternoon. Recently I had used my free time to write a short story, and I was considering the idea of trying to find a publisher. It had always been my dream to be a writer, and I had even won a few contests when I was in school. But this was a new type of story for me. It was the true account of that moment in time when God had saved my life as I faced my grandfather's loaded gun.

"It's called '*Angels*'" Handing the manuscript to Phil that evening, I tried to act nonchalant as he began to read. I busied myself folding clothes from the basket of laundry that sat in front of me, occasionally stealing glances at my husband. It seemed he was deliberately keeping his face impassive and my nerves began to stretch; this was the first time I had ever shared my writing with him.

"I like it." Phil handed the manuscript to me and gave me a hug. "Good work." He reached for the television remote but I forestalled him.

"Um, there's more." Phil watched me warily. I didn't blame him, really. In the past few months we had discussed some major life-changes, and he knew me well enough that this sounded like another.

"I want to send it to a publisher." Phil looked relieved and reached for the remote again.

"Sounds good to me. It doesn't cost anything to do that, right?" I shook my head and then plunged on. "I think God is calling me to be a writer."

Phil looked confused for a moment and then understanding dawned. "You mean as opposed to being employed?" He won the brief struggle for the remote and suddenly the television screen was filled with the crew of the Starship Enterprise. "I thought we agreed that you were going to work full-time to help save for the house and the adoption. Are you changing the plan now?" The words were clipped.

"No. I don't know." I stood restlessly and settled the

laundry basket at my waist. "I'm not planning to quit any-time soon, of course, but I can't shake this feeling that my writing is part of the adoption process. Maybe God wants to use the income to help pay for the adoption. Can we just pray about what this might mean?"

"No." Phil turned to face me. "I'll need some proof," he said. "This is the deal. For now you will keep your job and you can write in your spare time. If, at the end of six months you have made six hundred dollars with your writing, then we can 'pray about it'." He turned up the volume on the television, listening as Mr. Spock tried to explain logic to Captain Kirk. The irony didn't escape me.

Logic. It seemed like most of our disagreements centered around that subject lately. I had often said that our marriage announcement should have said, "Pollyanna marries Mr. Spock." In many ways Phil and I were polar opposites, with Phil taking what he called the rational approach, while I tended to follow my discernment and what I sensed God might be saying. That didn't mean that Phil couldn't hear God, too, but I knew that on this particular subject, his mind was made up.

Six hundred dollars in six months? So far I had received a whopping seven dollars for my writing, and that was in junior high school. I had read enough writers magazines to know that it could take years to find a publisher for even the smallest article or story. While I recognized that Phil's approach was logical and reasonable, I was disappointed that he had immediately centered on the monetary aspect of my writing "career". I had tried to explain my heart for a ministry, while his mind was focused on a job. Once again, Mr. Spock and Pollyanna were at odds.

I gathered up the pages of my story and settled at the kitchen table to look over the information in the Writer's Market I had brought home from the library. It didn't take long to realize that earning six hundred dollars in six months would be a major undertaking. An hour later I had chosen three publishers to send my story and had prepared my manuscript according to their specifications. As I headed out to the post office, I glanced at the calendar on the kitchen wall. It was the third week of January. I had six months.

July 1987

"That's beautiful Debbi. Is it new?" My friend, Judy, smoothed the soft fabric of my green skirt.

"Oh, I have had it for a few weeks. Phil insisted that I use my first writing check just on myself, so I bought it with some of the money." I smiled as I watched Phil on the stage warming up with the worship team. Phil had been almost as excited as I was when I received a check in the mail for "*Angels*" from the first publisher I had contacted. But, he continued to remind me that I still had several hundred dollars to earn, and time was running out. Three more short stories and articles had sold in the past few months, but the payment was small, and I was beginning to wonder if I could meet the challenge. I reassured myself that the agreement with Phil was just that, between us. God seemed to be blessing my writing even beyond my expectations. I had even heard Him say that these were the 'first fruits' of my writing. Although I wasn't sure what that meant, it seemed to indicate more success to come. I was satisfied, even if I didn't make the deadline, but it would have been nice to have the validation that I had, indeed, heard God.

A few days later, when Phil asked me how much money I had made so far, I had to confess that I was still two hundred dollars short of the goal. A few more items had gone out to publishers, but I knew it would take a miracle and several large sales to make that much money in the next two weeks. I spent the morning with my housework, and occupied my mind with my next writing project. As I was sitting down to lunch, the kitchen phone rang.

"Is this Debbi Migit?" I didn't recognize the voice, and the accent had a decidedly New York inflection.

"Yes, may I help you?" I automatically prepared my 'we do not purchase from phone solicitors' speech.

"My name is Deirdre Lang from Reader's Digest. I wanted to speak with you about the item you recently submitted to us. We would like to publish it in our magazine." I clutched the phone tighter and tried to sound professional.

"That sounds wonderful."

My mother had told the story to me, and when I submitted it to Reader's Digest, I had insisted that I wanted to share with her any payment I might receive. As Ms. Lang continued to discuss the publishing process, I quickly added up the total. Reader's Digest paid three hundred dollars for those items, so my half would be one hundred fifty dollars. I was so close to the goal. Ms. Lang explained that I would receive a check and a copy of the magazine from them by the following week.

Thanking Ms. Lang, I hung up the phone. Fifty dollars. That was the amount I now needed to meet the goal Phil had set for me. I quickly found my writing notebook and began the project I had been thinking of that morning. Two days later I submitted that story and went to work on the next, but as the days wore on, I began to realize that I would most likely not reach the goal. Phil had long since abandoned his hard stand on the subject and even surprised me with a new typewriter. He was solidly behind my writing now, but I still heard the challenge ringing in my ears. And for some reason, I sensed God had heard it, too. It seemed that there was more at stake here than if I earned a certain amount of money. I began to believe that God was in the process of proving to Phil and me that He would supply our needs if we remained obedient. I knew this lesson was one that would take us through business struggles, adoption fears, and beyond.

It seemed fitting that the check from Reader's Digest arrived on the very day the six month deadline expired. I tore open the envelope and saw that a note was attached to the check. It was from Ms. Lang, once again congratulating me on my sale. The last sentence caught my attention. "I am also pleased to inform you that, starting with this issue, our magazine will be paying four hundred dollars for personal stories such as yours." I looked down at the check in my hand. Four hundred dollars. Even after sharing half with my mother, I had still met the challenge; to the penny and to the day. I rushed inside to show Phil the check, not realizing that God had even bigger plans and purposes for my writing.

Chapter Thirteen

July 1986

The little yellow house appeared deserted as I pulled into the drive. My appointment with the bank representative was scheduled for 2:00 pm., but I had arrived a few minutes early. I studied the house. The raised, ranch style offered a walk-out basement; there was a nice deck attached off the kitchen area. A large back yard was home to a big maple tree and several small hills. I liked a yard with character. The surrounding houses were far apart, giving the area almost a rural feel. Bittersweet Lane. It seemed like we'd been living on Bittersweet Lane for a long time; we might as well make it official.

A car pulled into the driveway behind me, and I climbed out of my VW to meet Mr. Owens from National Bank. My heart began to pound, and I hoped Mr. Owens couldn't hear it. Trying to act nonchalant, I offered my hand in greeting, but inside I was a jumble of excitement and nerves. I had called Mr. Owens about the little house on Bittersweet Lane after I saw the *FOR SALE* sign in the front yard. After explaining that the house had been repossessed, he had agreed to give me a tour.

As we walked up the deck and entered the kitchen, I mentally ran the floor plan in my head. I knew this house. Two years earlier, I had come to an open house here and had fallen in love. We had just started the fertility treatments, and I was sure that this was the house where we would bring our new baby. Everything was just what I had dreamed of for our first home. Unfortunately, the price had been a nightmare. Another family had purchased "the little yellow house," as I had come to think of it, and Phil and I continued to rent our duplex. But I often took a detour down Bittersweet Lane, just because something about the house made me smile. Maybe it was the cheerful yellow color, or the white shutters, or even the matching yellow barn at the end of the driveway. Whatever it was, the house on Bittersweet Lane had become a familiar place to me.

"I apologize for the condition of the house," Mr. Owens was saying as I took my first look around the kitchen. "It has been empty for several weeks now, but we just put the *For Sale* sign up yesterday. You are the first person to call about it." Mr. Owens crossed to the living room and opened the front door to let in some fresh air. The house had been well cared for, and I felt a pang of grief for the family who had been forced to re-locate due to a lost job. Mr. Owens led me through the living room to the sleeping area.

"This is the master bedroom, bath, and a second bedroom," he said. "Do you have children?"

An enigmatic smile accompanied my answer. "Eventually."

I stepped into the smaller bedroom and allowed myself a quick daydream. This would be the nursery. The white walls would be accented with bright, primary colors, something cheerful and vibrant.

The lower level of the house was a surprise. I had forgotten how large the family room was and that it included a brick hearth and wood burning stove. Another bedroom, bath, and laundry room finished up the lower level and we walked out through the attached garage.

"Do you think you and your husband would be interested?" Mr. Owens asked as we returned to our cars. My heart began its tattoo again. Now was the moment of truth.

"When I called the bank, I was told a price hadn't been determined yet." I replied. "That will certainly affect our decision." Mr. Owens looked flustered for a minute and then reached for his briefcase.

"Of course," he said as he opened the case and removed some papers. "I just left a meeting this morning where we were determining the prices for several properties we have re-acquired recently. We agreed that these houses need to have new owners as soon as possible, so we have set the prices accordingly." He handed me a paper with a picture of the house and information. At the top was printed the asking price. My hands trembled as I read and re-read the numbers. Two years earlier, we had been unable to purchase the house because it was out of our price range. Our income had grown since then as our auto-body business had become more established. Phil and I had agreed that if the amount was near the asking price of two years earlier, we might make an offer. But the number I was reading could not be right. The bank was selling the house for almost twenty thousand dollars less than the house had appraised and sold for two years earlier!

Mr. Owens must have misinterpreted the look of disbelief on my face.

"It really is a fair price," he defended. "And we would be willing to be flexible on a down-payment, if you qualify." Ah, the down-payment, another problem.

"Um, how flexible?" I asked, barely glancing up from the numbers printed on the page. I was almost afraid if I looked away, the price would change. Mr. Owens hadn't reached an executive position at National bank without being able to read people.

"How much down payment do you have?" he asked. I looked up at him.

"We have invested everything back into our business," I said quietly. "We don't have much for a down payment."

"How much?"

"None." Mr. Owens studied me for a minute, and I thought I saw his lips twitch in a small smile.

"Closing costs would be four hundred dollars," he said gently.

"We can handle that," I assured him, stunned that I wasn't seeing the taillights of his Lincoln as he spun off.

"Mrs. Migit, if your income and credit history qualify you, it's a deal." Mr. Owens held out his hand and gave mine a firm shake. "Why don't you call my office and make an appointment with my secretary. You and your husband can come in and we will begin the paperwork. We have been moving quickly on these houses, so you should expect an answer within a few days, and since the house is empty, you could even move in within six weeks. How does that sound?"

Miraculous, I thought as I drove away. *It sounded miraculous.*

Chapter Fourteen

OCTOBER 1987

Glancing down at the scribbled directions on the page next to me, I muttered, "Turn left on Illinois and then right on McArthur." I had left our home, the little yellow house on Bittersweet Lane, in plenty of time for the appointment. In a way I had been headed for this appointment for eighteen months; it wouldn't do to be late now.

Approaching the intersection, I tried to read the street sign. Unfortunately, wind and time had taken their toll; while the pole still stood, the street name was nowhere to be seen. I turned left and glanced at the clock on my dashboard. My appointment with the adoption agency was in five minutes. My fear of being late joined in the jumble of other feelings. There was excitement, hope, and a very real terror of being denied by the agency. The woman I had spoken with on the phone had seemed very friendly and accessible, but I was still not sure if the Catholic Social Service would be open to placing a baby with a couple who was not Catholic. I wondered how I would answer when the inevitable question came, "Are you a member of a church?"

Phil and I were certainly church members; I just wasn't sure if anyone in the Catholic Social Service had ever heard of the Vineyard church before. When Phil and I made the decision to help plant a Vineyard in our town, even my parents were questioning. What was The Vineyard? I had been raised in the Assemblies of God, and I tried to explain to my parents that our beliefs were still the same, but Phil and I were drawn to the more casual setting that the Vineyard offered. We also appreciated the new style of worship and were very involved in leading the worship band every Sunday. We loved our church, but I just didn't know if I could explain it to the caseworker.

As I drove, I practiced my answers to her inevitable questions. How long had we been married? Nine years. Were we employed? Yes, we owned our own auto body business and had five employees. Yes, we had been homeowners for four months. No, I would not be working outside the home after the baby came. My freelance writing continued to generate some income, and I was excited to be able to work from home. Yes, our families were supportive of our decision to adopt transracially. Yes, we would be willing to take the recommended classes.

As my mind raced, I drove slower, trying to locate Illinois Street. I had already gone farther on this road than the directions showed, and the fear of being lost was a growing concern. A woman was jogging toward me along the side of the road and slowing down, I lowered my window.

"Excuse me," I said. "Is this Illinois?"

The woman continued to jog in place as she studied me for a moment. Finally, she gave a brief nod of her head and answered, "Well, yes, it is." Then she raced off.

Calling out a thank you, I drove on. I looked for my turn on McArthur. Puzzled, I studied the street sign at the intersection. I was already on McArthur, not Illinois as the jogger had assured me. In fact, the Catholic Social Services office was right in front of me. Parking the car, I replayed my brief conversation with the jogger. Now, why would she give me wrong information? A glance back at the jogger showed that she was shaking her head as she ran, and suddenly I realized: she thought I was so lost I didn't even know which state I was in! My brief laugh distracted me for a few moments, but when I was finally ushered into the meeting room, the butterflies were back.

"Just have a seat Mrs. Migit, and Andrea will be with you in a few moments." The secretary indicated that I should sit at the long table that dominated the room, and then she left, closing the door with a small click. Doubts flooded my mind and I almost stood up to slip out the back door. *How could I be sure that this was the right step for us to take?* Adoption would surely bring its own issues, but adding the challenges of transracial adoption suddenly seemed overwhelming. *Could we do it? How could I know that we would be the kind of parents this child would need?*

"Father," I whispered. "Please give me peace and reassure me that this is of You." I thought again of my concerns about how the Vineyard church might be viewed. It was such a new and small association, the caseworker would be well within her rights to question its validity. "Lord, I am asking for a sign, just between us. If adoption is truly Your plan for Phil and me, please give me the words to explain to Andrea about our church affiliation. Let her accept it, and us." I barely had time to finish the words when the door opened and a young woman entered.

"Mrs. Migit, I am Andrea Baker, and I will be your caseworker if you decide to pursue adoption through our agency." Andrea was a lovely blonde woman in her late twenties, and I immediately felt at ease with her. As we began to discuss the details of adoption I quickly learned that the agency was actively searching for adoptive parents for African American children.

"Frankly, the state was against transracial adoption for many years," Andrea explained. "Many African American children spent their whole childhood in foster care, because the state was not willing to place them permanently with Caucasian parents. Thankfully, that view has changed, and we will be willing to help you in any way we can to make the adoption process go smoothly. You and your husband will attend several classes that we offer on transracial adoption, and we will meet with you to work on your home study."

"When do the classes start?" I asked.

"Well, I'm afraid the next series of classes won't begin until April of next year." Andrea said apologetically. My heart fell.

"But, the good news is that while you are taking the classes, we will be working on your home study, and I can safely say that you will most likely have a baby by the end of next year." I tried to act calm as I responded.

"That sounds wonderful." On one hand it did; after ten years of waiting, hoping, and praying, what was another year? But there were some days when my heart and arms ached so badly I thought I would die if I had to wait another day.

Andrea seemed to read my thoughts, because she said gently, "There will be so much to do that should make the time go faster. We will definitely do our best to keep you busy!"

"Now," Andrea continued as she looked at her notebook. "I just have a few more important questions to ask you. I see that you marked on the questionnaire that you are not Catholic. Can you tell me what your church affiliation is?" *Here it comes,* I thought as I tried to remember the little speech I had rehearsed on the way over.

"Well, Phil and I are very active in our church," I began. "But I'm just not sure if it is a church you might have heard of before." Andrea raised an eyebrow and waited for me to continue. I remembered my request earlier that God would show me if adoption was His choice for us. I had specifically asked Him to help the caseworker accept our church, even though it was not well known.

"What is the name of your church?" Andrea asked with her pen poised over the notebook.

"Um, it's called the Vineyard." I held my breath and then was dismayed as Andrea's head came up and she looked intently at me.

"Did you say the Vineyard?" Andrea spoke the words urgently and my heart began to pound. Andrea put down her pen, stood up, and walked toward me. Tears gathered in my eyes as I imagined our hopes of adoption stopping right here and now. I had asked God for an answer if this was His will. I just wished He would have told me before I had been promised a baby within a year. Andrea approached me and leaned over, looking me in the eyes.

"Are you saying you attend a Vineyard church? Here in this area?" I nodded and found my voice.

"Phil and I are part of a church plant. We have been there for about two years." I watched in shock as Andrea began to weep softly. She sat next to me and took my hand.

"I'm sorry to be acting this way," she apologized. "But I just moved here a few months ago from California." She smiled softly as she added, "I became a Christian at the original Vineyard in California. John Wimber was my pastor," she said, naming the man who had started the Vineyard movement. "I have been so homesick," she continued. "Just this morning, I was begging God to bring someone that I could talk to that would understand how much I miss my church home. When you said what church you belong to, I was overwhelmed by God's faithfulness to me. Please, tell me about yourself."

An hour later I left the Catholic Social Services office with a large packet of information and something I hadn't expected. I had a new sister in the Lord.

Chapter Fifteen

April 1988

The whirring of the vacuum drowned out the songs of the birds that were making a nest outside my living room window. Opening the front door, I let in a little of the spring breeze, even though it was still cool in Illinois for the beginning of April. My mind was whirring as hard as the vacuum as I considered the classes Phil and I would start attending in a few weeks. Even though it was still months before I could finally hold our baby, my pulse quickened as I thought about the child God had told us was coming. Over the past few months since my meeting with Andrea, I had spent a lot of time praying about the baby. I had specific requests that I asked for almost every day. Today was no different and I began my prayer list as I pushed the vacuum around our small living room.

"Lord, you know that we trust you to bring us exactly the child you have picked for us. But I also believe you have given me specific things to pray for, and I want to be obedient. So, Lord, first I am asking that the birthmother of this child would be a Christian." Every time I spoke that prayer, my heart would drop a little. I realized that most Christian girls who discovered they were pregnant either married the father or kept the baby themselves. I felt like I was lowering our chances of receiving a baby by making that particular request. But I continued to pray what I felt was God's heart for our situation. "I also ask that the birthmother would not be a teenager. Let her be old enough and mature enough to make an adult decision. Please God, spare us the anguish of a birthmother who changes her mind. Bless her and the baby with health. And Lord," I hesitated a moment at this step, just as I always did. It seemed like such a big thing to ask. "Lord, I ask that she would pray over this baby that she is carrying, so that he would not feel rejected. Let him know he is loved by her and us, even in the womb. Bless her Lord and give her peace during this time. Let her know that you are in control of her life and of the life of this child that she is carrying. Thank You, Father, for your faithfulness."

The vacuum had long since been turned off, and I sank to the couch as I poured out my heart. I had been praying this same prayer for months, but today I felt urged to add something new.

"Father, I'm not sure what this means, but although I know the child you have for us is African American, I suddenly also feel a longing for a child that is Native American." I jumped up in excitement. Maybe God was planning to give us two babies! Glancing around our small living room, I imagined bringing two babies into our home at one time. They would almost be like twins. I smiled at the thought. Since I was a twin myself and had five sets in my immediate family, I had always thought twins would be wonderful. I knew of people who had adopted one child and then immediately been offered another baby. I wasn't sure what this new prayer meant, but I knew it was from God's heart.

What would Phil say if I told him we might get two babies at one time? My excitement quickly carried me through my chores, and I was just folding the last bath towel when I heard the still, small voice of the Lord, whispering to my heart.

"*Call Catholic Social Services and cancel the adoption. Your child won't be coming through them.*" The words were so real and unexpected my knees buckled. I slipped onto the couch. *Cancel the adoption? No!* That couldn't have been God speaking those words. I immediately began to pray and tell the enemy to leave me alone and stop lying to me. But even as I prayed, I knew the truth. As unwelcome as those words were, there was also a peace that accompanied them. This was God, and I knew I had a choice. *Would I obey and trust Him, or try and make this dream come true my own way?*

Over the years I had learned to recognize that voice. Times of direction and protection flashed through my mind as I weighed the enormity of my decision. But in all of the times that I had been faced with the choice of obedience, this was the most difficult decision of my life. I began to cry.

"Ten years, God! We have waited ten long years and now we are so close. Why are you doing this? Have I failed you somehow? Won't I be a good mother? I don't understand." I crumpled to the floor as I let my anguish pour out. The afternoon shadows lengthened as I prayed. And in the end, I knew what had to be done. My dream of holding our baby in my arms slipped away as I picked up the phone and told Phil what I head heard. But even in my heartbreak, there was peace. Phil heard me out, and as he often did, spoke just the right words to raise my faith again.

"God said the baby isn't coming through this agency. He didn't say the baby isn't coming at all. And I have to tell you, I've been hearing the same thing for a few weeks myself."

"But why didn't you tell me?" I whispered.

"I knew that if I was right, God would tell you Himself. And that you would accept it a lot better from Him than from me." Peace surrounded me as I made the call to Catholic Social Services. I might not understand what was happening, but there was one thing I was sure of; God was in control.

Tuesday was my favorite day of the week, because that was when our church's Bible study group met. Phil always took his guitar and led worship, and I loved the time of sharing and fellowship with some of our closest friends. It had been three weeks since we had cancelled the adoption, and I had to admit, my faith was becoming a little shaky.

As we greeted our friends Jeff and Terri, Jeff asked if we had any more news about the adoption.

"No, we are just waiting to see what God has planned next." My response was spoken softly.

Jeff leaned toward me and said, "Have you considered that maybe this isn't God's plan or timing for you? I mean, first you focused on fertility treatments for several years and nothing came of that. And now it seems that maybe adoption isn't going to happen either. Terri and I are becoming concerned about you, Debbi. We think maybe you need to stop being so obsessed with having a child. You and Phil have some wonderful gifts that God could use on the mission field. You could try for a promotion in your job or maybe go back to school. Terri and I thought that you might also consider counseling to help you let go of your obsession."

I looked over at Jeff's wife, Terri, who was pregnant with their fourth child. Angry words burned on my tongue, but were quickly swallowed as hurt washed over me. My friends pitied me. They thought I had an unhealthy obsession; they didn't believe the promise I had heard from God. Looking around the room I wondered how many other friends were thinking the same thing. Jeff had been spending more time with Phil lately, and suddenly I understood my husband's recent change of attitude. Although Phil agreed that we had made the right decision in canceling our plans with

Catholic Social Service, he had become more withdrawn and reluctant to talk about a baby. Stifling a sob, I realized I had never felt so alone in my life. Even my husband thought I was wrong.

Somehow I managed to find a secluded place in the corner and was relieved as the worship music began. Ducking my head so no one could see my tears, I silently poured out my pain.

"God, I don't understand. Jeff and Terri have been so supportive of us all along. Why have they changed? And even Phil won't discuss the adoption unless I really press the issue. My faith gets tested at times, but God, I think this may be more than I can take. I have loved and respected Jeff and Terri for a long time, and we have been through so much together." I scooted back a little closer to the wall, so the others couldn't hear me crying over the sound of the music. Even more devastating than my friend's words was the thought that they might be right. *What if I had spent all this time praying and believing for something that just wasn't in God's plan?* It broke my heart to think that I had wasted all these years, when we might have pursued a ministry that God could bless. *What if I was a disappointment to God? What if I really was obsessed?*

The strumming of Phil's guitar seemed more distant now. For a moment I was in a place and time alone with God, waiting for Him to speak. And He did.

"*Daughter, what they call obsession, I call faith.*" My breath caught as I grasped the significance of those words.

I was not a disappointment to Him. I was not disobedient. The reality of God's love and approval washed over me and began take away the sting of hurt. I realized there was nothing I could say to my friends or even my husband that could convince them that this was truly of God. I just had to trust Him to vindicate me when the time was right. Moving back to join the group, I began to sing. It was time to worship.

Chapter Sixteen

MAY 19, 1988

Several weeks had passed since that night at the Bible study, and I had spent a lot of time praying to release my hurt and anger towards my friends. Our worship ministry and my job at the insurance agency kept me busy. The issue of adoption was seldom mentioned anymore, and Phil seemed relieved. But inside, something was stirring in me.

One night after Phil went to bed, I took my Bible into the living room to read and pray. I sat on the floor next to our beautiful cradle that had been a surprise birthday gift from our Bible study group a few months earlier. Opening my Bible I found myself caught up in the story of Joshua and the children of Israel walking around the city of Jericho. The scriptures ignited in my heart, and strangely, I felt compelled to walk around the cradle seven times. I placed it in the middle of the room and began the walk, declaring as I went that God's promises were true and that He had given us that cradle in preparation for the child to come. I asked God to fill it. It was about 1:00 am, so I tried to be very quiet, since Phil was sleeping in the next room.

Finishing the seventh circuit, I prayed one more time, giving the future to the Lord. For the first time in weeks, I slept peacefully.

The next morning I tried to keep busy with housework, but as the morning wore on, I became more agitated. Finally, I could stand it no longer. I finished making the bed and then sank down on the quilted bedspread that Phil's grandmother had made for us. My tears fell as I cried, "God, we obeyed you! We turned down the only real opportunity we have had in ten years, because I know that You told me our baby isn't coming that way. But Father, I'm almost out of hope. Please tell me, when will we have the child you have promised?"

2 Kings 4:16. My sobs quieted as I heard the whisper repeat in my heart. 2 Kings 4:16. The ticking of the clock was the only sound as I held my breath and listened. 2 Kings 4:16. For the third time, the Scripture reference whispered in my consciousness. Slowly reaching to the nightstand, I gathered up my Bible. The Scripture was unfamiliar to me, but I ruffled the pages and quickly found it.

"Then he said, "about this time next year you will embrace your son." And she said, "No my lord, Man of God, do not lie to your maidservant" (2 Kings 4:16, NKJV).

The tiny hairs stood up on my arms as I read the verse again and again.

"*About this time next year, you will embrace your son.*" My mind raced back to my earlier question, "When, God?" Apparently, I had my answer.

I stayed there on the floor for hours that afternoon. Alternately laughing and crying, I reviewed my history with God; how He sometimes spoke to me in ways that seemed extraordinary. Even as a child I had loved to climb up in my favorite tree and talk to God about everything. I just expected Him to talk back; after all it was only polite! As I grew up, I began to treasure those precious times of communion and conversation. I also asked God to train me how to hear His voice more clearly and especially asked Him to guard me from presumption. I was so blessed to grow up in a Christian home, where listening to God was valued; my church had also taught me to weigh anything I thought I heard from God against the Scriptures. Now I realized how valuable my heritage was; it gave me the faith to believe that God could do anything. But experience had also taught me another lesson. Always before a victory came a test. As I knelt on the floor that day, I wondered what might come that would test the wonderful promise I had just been given.

July 1988

"Oh, this is so cute!" I said, holding up the baby blanket to show my friend Judy. It was Wednesday, and we were enjoying one of our favorite pastimes—garage sales. Judy smiled tentatively and then tried to direct my attention to the house-wares section of the driveway. I knew I was confusing my friend, but I couldn't help myself. Hugging my secret closer, I put the baby blanket in my stack of items to purchase. Ever since that day, May 19, 1988, as I often thought of it, I had been buying a few baby items to tuck away for the time I would need them. I knew it was still early; our baby wouldn't be born until May nineteenth of next year, but I couldn't resist a few little things. I looked through the stacks of baby boy clothing on the table in front of me.

That day, as I knelt on the floor, God had finally given me what I asked. Not only did He tell me that we would have a boy, He said that He was being specific about the timing. I had immediately found my prayer journal and written down the scripture and the date. *On May 19, 1988, God told me that in exactly one year I will embrace our son.* I had also been instructed not to tell anyone, not even Phil. The idea that I was obsessed continued to sting, and I knew that this instruction was a protection for me. I was uncertain just how this child would come, through birth or adoption, but it truly didn't matter to me. All I knew was that God himself had promised us a son, and I finally believed Him.

As I paid for my purchases, I decided not to worry Judy any more that day by buying baby clothes. It was tempting to purchase maternity clothes instead, but I knew that would be presumption on my part. Although I knew to the day when I would conceive to deliver on May nineteenth, I was unsure if this would be a birth child. There were still dreams of that beautiful little boy who floated in the clouds, and I knew he could only come through adoption. I was content to wait and see what the future would bring.

Chapter Seventeen

SEPTEMBER 29, 1988

I carefully placed a pink bow on the package I was wrapping. Baby showers were often bittersweet for me, and I didn't expect this one to be any different. The time had come and gone for me to conceive if I was to deliver next May. I wasn't pregnant and I was starting to feel my faith wavering. For a moment, I considered staying home from the shower, but I truly wanted to rejoice with my friend, Kathy, on the birth of her new daughter. Pushing the sadness away, I was determined to have a good time. Besides, I reasoned, there would be cake.

The church fellowship hall was filled with old friends that I hadn't seen in years. I made the circuit, sharing hugs, until I saw a special person who was waving to me.

"Pam!" I leaned down to kiss her cheek and sat in the chair next to her. Pam and her husband, Ben, had encouraged us years ago in our pursuit of adoption. They had adopted nine children themselves and for a time even had a ministry to birthmothers, giving them a home as they awaited their delivery time. Pam held a special place in my heart and I was thrilled to see her again. Pam's eyes twinkled as she skipped the small talk and got right to the point.

"I have a baby for you." Pam's statement was so matter of fact I began to look around, half expecting to see a baby carrier next to her.

"Huh?" I had always expected that when the moment finally came, I would be more eloquent. Apparently not.

"He's not born yet," Pam leaned over and whispered. "But he is yours. All you have to do is say, 'yes'." Again, words eluded me. Pam must have taken my dropped jaw for a sign to continue.

"There is a young woman named Holly, who is living with us right now. She is pregnant and is due in six weeks. She has heard about you and Phil and your desire to adopt a baby, and she said that God has told her that she is carrying your son. As you might guess from that, Holly is a Christian. She is in her early 20s and has taken a leave of absence from college to carry the baby. You don't need to worry about health problems; her major is in nutrition, and she has never smoked or taken drugs." Pam continued as if she had no idea she was reading my prayer list. "You do need to consider this." Pam watched me intently. "This would be a transracial adoption. The baby's birthfather is African American, and Holly is part Native American." Somewhere across the room laughter echoed as shower games were played and gifts were opened.

I managed to smile and nod as people greeted me, but inside I was in shock. I wanted to jump for joy and weep all at the same time. My emotions were a jumble of excitement and even a bit of fear. *A baby in six weeks? I wasn't ready!* I disregarded the fact I had literally been preparing for this since the day I said "I do" ten years earlier. But in the midst of the thrill of knowing I would soon—finally—hold our child, there was another emotion. I was overcome with awe that God had answered every request on my prayer list— even to the fact that the baby was African American *and* Native American. There was only one request that had not been granted, and I had always known that was unlikely. As the shower ended I said my "goodbyes" and promised Pam I would call her as soon as I spoke with Phil.

"Oh wait, there is one more thing I forgot to tell you." Pam caught my hand as I started to leave.

"As soon as Holly found out she was pregnant, a friend gave her a book titled *Praying for Your Unborn Child.* She has prayed over this baby every day in the womb, asking God that he would not feel abandoned or rejected because of her decision to make an adoption plan. Holly says she knows this is your son, and she asks God every day to bless him, and you too."

Tears blinded my eyes as I drove home. The afternoon had taken on an almost surreal quality. I wasn't sure how much more I could absorb. Phil was relaxing on the couch, and I knelt down beside him.

"Hi, how was the shower?" He quickly sat up as he saw my tears, assuming the celebration had been too painful for me. Shaking my head, I tried to gather myself to coherently share the news.

"Phil, it's finally time. Our baby is coming!" I carefully explained everything that Pam had told me about Holly. As I reached out for my husband, I was thrilled that the growing distance between us would finally be closed. Phil stared at me for a moment and then stood to begin pacing the room.

"What did you tell her? You didn't make any promises did you?"

"No, of course not. I told her we would pray about it and let her know as soon as possible. But Phil, this has to be our baby! Everything on my prayer list has been answered." I watched in disbelief as Phil's expression turned stony.

"That's great for you," he stated. "Now you can start on my list!" Then he walked out the door.

Chapter Eighteen

"Debbi?" Pam's voice sounded concerned. "Did you hear what I said?" Tightening my grip on the telephone, I responded.

"Yes, I heard you. We need to give you our decision in two days. I understand."

"Debbi, it's been almost four weeks since I told you about the baby. Frankly, I expected you to say yes immediately. Is it the race difference that is concerning you?" Tears slowed my speech for a moment, and then I was able to answer with complete truthfulness.

"No, that's not it at all. We have believed for quite some time that our baby would be African American. That's not the problem."

"Then what is it?" She persisted. "There are only two more weeks until the due date, and sometimes babies come early, you know? If you and Phil decide this baby is not for you, then Holly needs to begin making another plan." My heart constricted as I thought of our baby going to another family.

Please, God, no! I cried inside. I managed to answer Pam with some measure of calm.

"We are still praying, that is all I can say right now. I will call you back on Thursday with our answer, I promise." Pam responded with the reminder of 'two more days' and then hung up.

Slumping at the kitchen table, I laid down my head. This couldn't be happening. *How could we be so close and yet so far from our dream?* I had told Pam the truth, though. Phil and I were still praying about the adoption, but we were praying different things.

The day of the shower I had told Phil about my conversation with Pam. When I explained all of my prayer requests and how each one had been met, I expected Phil to run to the phone and give Pam and Ben a resounding *Yes.*

Instead he said nothing. Phil insisted that I say nothing, either. He said he needed to be able to hear God on his own terms. That was fine, but I had waited four long weeks in silence, and Phil still would not make the commitment. Each passing day seemed to pull us farther apart until I not only feared losing the baby, I was beginning to fear for my marriage.

I went to the family room to pace and pray; I was doing a lot of both these days. There were so many things to do to prepare for the baby. Months earlier I had purchased a used crib, and it was stored in the garage with a meager supply of baby items. I didn't dare begin to prepare the nursery, because Phil had told me that any gesture like that would feel like pressure to him. Phil had agreed to receive prayer counseling from some friends from our church. It was difficult to find people who were willing to meet with him, because he was becoming increasingly angry. Just two days earlier, Phil had almost come to blows with a friend who had tried to talk to him about the adoption. I knew that the wrong word could close his mind and heart forever. So I had to be content with crying out to God all day, and then trying to maintain a quiet spirit at night. It was the hardest thing I had ever done.

"I don't want it to be like this, you know," Phil had told me just that morning. "I want us to be able to take this baby. But there is something inside of me that just won't let me say yes. It has nothing to do with adoption or race, and everything to do with me. I don't know if I can be a good father. I don't know if I can open up to love another person, knowing that he might be taken from me. You slipped through my defenses. I just can't make myself that vulnerable again."

I had come to realize that the only thing that was going to break this deadlock was prayer. I was cautious about asking God to change Phil's mind and had instead been praying for my husband to be freed from whatever was keeping him in an emotional prison. It was my experience that memories, long buried, could affect our emotions in powerful ways. Although I believed that God could heal whatever hurt was associated with this fear, I was also very aware of our time limitations. We only had two more days.

As I sat and rocked, I began to feel the calming presence of the Holy Spirit. And then God's voice began to capture my thoughts.

Debbi, do you remember how Jack was before he accepted Me? I was startled by the question. Jack was part of our fellowship now, but several years earlier he had worked for us at the auto body shop. He had not been a Christian at the time, and there were many Mondays when he came to work nursing bruises from a weekend bar fight. One Friday night, he accepted Jesus as his personal Savior, and the next Sunday morning when he had walked into our church, I could hardly believe my eyes. I had never seen anyone change so much, almost overnight. He looked fifteen years younger, and so happy and free.

Tonight, I am going to do a radical change in Phil; it will be as dramatic as the change you witnessed in Jack. God's assurance began to sooth my spirit.

"But how, Lord?" I questioned. The answer was brief. *Trust Me.*

That evening when Phil came home from work, I held my breath, expecting to see the miracle I had been promised. Instead I saw the same anger and frustration of the past four weeks, and my heart broke.

Hanging up his coat Phil said, "This is the last chance."

"What do you mean?" I questioned.

"I called George and Alice," Phil said, naming some friends from church. "They agreed to meet with me one more time to pray about the baby." Phil held up his hand as he saw my excitement.

"No, wait. I am only doing this because I love you, and I know I have to try one more time. But after tonight, I never want you to ask me about adoption again. Unless God does a miracle tonight, the subject is closed, forever."

Suddenly, the words I had heard earlier in the afternoon took on a new urgency. My heart pounded as I prepared a quick dinner so Phil could leave for the meeting. We barely spoke during the meal and a few minutes later, he was gone. I didn't even take the time to clean the dishes, but just raced to the family room for my Bible. For over an hour I poured out my heart and heartbreak to God. I had seen so many miracles already, but this just seemed too hard. The strong fears and emotions Phil was facing had been buried for years. *How could God change his heart so quickly?* My faith was stretched to the limit, and finally, I slid into the chair, exhausted. I had prayed everything I knew to pray, and now I let the Spirit pray through me. There was nothing to do now but wait.

Three hours passed. Suddenly I heard Phil's footsteps on the stairs and my heart began to pound. As he entered the room I realized that I had never seen my husband look so solemn.

Sitting on the couch next to me, Phil took my hand and asked gently, "Is it too late to call Pam tonight?" I shook my head and waited for his next words.

"Good, because we need to tell her as soon as possible."

For the first time in a month I saw my husband's smile come through. "We're ready for our baby." Joy leapt in me and I began to cry.

"How?" was all I could ask. Phil shook his head to indicate he wasn't sure himself.

"All I know is, when I left here tonight, I was determined to get this over with and return to our life. As hard as I've prayed these past few weeks, and I have prayed," he assured me, "I just could not feel peace about the adoption. I was afraid I would be a terrible father, and I was afraid that we would get the baby and he would be taken away by the birthmother. I guess the point is, I was afraid of being hurt."

"But what changed?" I asked.

"At first, nothing. Everyone was praying for me, but I was emotionally numb. I began to think that it was just a waste of time. But as soon as that thought came, George spoke up and said, 'I take authority over the thought that this is a waste of time'." Phil gave a rueful laugh.

"That got my attention. Then they asked God to show me why I was having such a hard time hearing Him on this subject. Suddenly, I saw a picture in my mind of an event that happened when I was a little boy. I was angry about something—I never did remember what, and I don't think it's important. But I saw myself running out the front door of the house where I grew up, slamming the door, and yelling, 'I don't need you; I don't need anybody!'"

Watching me, Phil continued, "when the memory came

back, so did the emotions, and I realized that is exactly what I have been feeling and saying these past few weeks. I had emotionally cut myself off and was refusing to open up to love anyone else. As soon as I asked God to break the power of those words, all of the fear and anger were gone. And suddenly, I knew that this is really our child. God is giving us a wonderful gift; I just can't believe I almost missed it!" Moments later we spoke to Pam and assured her that we were thrilled to be able to say yes.

It was almost midnight when I finally settled down to sleep. My mind was a whirl of thoughts; I had so many things to do in the next two weeks. But more than anything, I was again in awe of my Lord's faithfulness. He truly did watch over His word to perform it.

Two weeks later...

"Hello, anybody home?"

"I'm back here, in the nursery!" My breath caught as I said those words; the nursery. The little bedroom was being transformed as I brought in my small supply of baby items. I had spent the morning happily arranging blankets and sleepers in the white dresser that had been mine as a child. The project was taking longer than I had planned, since daydreaming seemed to be a significant part of the ritual.

But I kept hearing Pam's words, "Babies can come early, you know." Although Holly wasn't due for ten more days, I wanted to be prepared. I was glad for the company now, though, because it was time to set up the crib. Rick and Sandy entered the room as I struggled to hang the curtains.

"Here, let me help you with that." Rick was well over six feet tall, so he had no trouble settling the curtain rod into the brackets. Sandy gave me a quick hug and then handed me a mobile of teddy bears.

"I wasn't sure if you had one," she said. "I brought some crib sheets and sleepers too, although, I left the pink ones at home."

"Thanks!" I took the items and resisted the temptation to sort through them. I loved touching the tiny sleepers and blankets that had started to accumulate around us.

"Well, what do you think?" I asked, gazing at the room in delight.

"I think you did the fun stuff and saved the hard stuff for us!" Rick said with a grin, indicating the white crib that lay in pieces in the corner. Sandy punched her husband's arm and laughed. "Hey, leave her alone, she's nesting. I think it's adorable!"

I studied the room and had to agree. White curtains fluttered in the breeze from the open window. Tiny, primary colored hearts danced across the fabric; the hearts matched the comforter and accessories that lay on the day bed in another corner of the room. Brightly colored, quilted balloons hung over the white dresser that would also serve as a changing table. Through the open closet door I could see the few tiny outfits that hung there, waiting.

"Hey, we brought you something else." Rick disappeared down the hall and then returned lugging a baby swing. "Can't have a baby without one of these things!" he declared as he set the swing up in the corner. He pressed a button and lilting music filled the room.

"Is this where the party is?" Soon our tiny living room was filled as more friends and family gathered throughout the day. Most stopped to drop off baby items, and stayed to pitch in with the work. By the time Phil arrived home that evening, the nursery was completed. Now all we needed was the baby.

We shared pizza with our decorating crew, and I was thrilled by the joy that echoed in our home. *What a difference!* I thought. Just two weeks earlier I had spent the day crying out to God, as Phil wrestled with this decision. Now my husband was laughing as our friends gave him parenting advice.

"Make sure you sleep as much as you can now, because you will never have another full night of sleep after the baby comes!" One by one our guests wandered into the nursery, just to sit and take it all in. Pillows were tossed on the floor as we made ourselves comfortable and a kind of holy silence settled on the room. Phil and Sandy brought in their guitars and soon sweet worship filled the nursery.

I love you Lord, and I lift my voice, to worship you,
Oh my soul rejoice,

Take joy my King in what You hear,
Let it be a sweet, sweet sound in your ear.

Tears wet my cheeks as we dedicated the nursery that night, and I realized, now we were ready.

Chapter Nineteen

"Hurry up, okay?" I watched the speedometer as we seemed to crawl down the road. Phil glanced at me and grinned.

"Would you mind speaking into the mic?" he asked, holding up an imaginary microphone. "I have to get this on tape. Aren't you the same lady that yells when I take the exit ramp too fast?" Ignoring that, I pointed to the books scattered on the seat between us.

"We don't have time for jokes." I said. "We have to name this baby! Maybe you should slow down so we have time to make up our minds. What will happen if we get to the hospital and we don't have a name picked out?" I glanced at the speedometer again and asked impatiently, "Can't you go any faster?"

Shaking his head, Phil suggested, "How about Saul Tobias? We can call him Salty for short." Since I had heard this comment many times in the past few weeks, I ignored him and picked up a book titled, *The A-Z book of Baby Names*. In the past six weeks since we had heard we would be parents, we had only made it through the letter N.

"You'd think that after ten years we would have this part figured out," I muttered, frantically flipping through the pages. Jane, our attorney, had told us that when we met her at the hospital we would first fill out some paperwork before we went to the nursery to get our son.

"You will need to have his name to put on the forms," she'd advised. My pulse pounded as I realized that in just moments I would finally hold my son, and I didn't even know his name!

The hospital parking lot was nearly empty, and Phil slid the station wagon into the closest space. Proudly, I took out the diaper bag I had purchased the day before. Our son had been born three days earlier, on his due date. It had been a Saturday, and Phil and I had spent the day shopping for baby equipment. We had returned home that evening, just as the phone began to ring.

"You have a healthy baby boy!" Pam's daughter, Cindy, had been in the delivery room with Holly, and she described our son as gorgeous. He weighed over nine pounds, and everything had gone perfectly. The next three days were the longest of my life—knowing our baby was just ten miles away in the hospital nursery, but unable to see him. Now, at last, the moment was here. If only we had a name! We entered the lobby and I pointed out a bench to Phil.

"Why don't you sit there for a few minutes and keep an eye out for Jane. I'm going to stop in the ladies room. And when we see each other again, we are going to tell the name we want for our baby. Let's just hope it's the same one!"

I entered the ladies room and stopped at the mirror. *The next time I see myself, I will be a Mommy,* I marveled.

Opening my purse, I removed a small piece of paper I had carried for the past six weeks. Names were scribbled all over, but suddenly I only saw one; I finally knew our son's name. I returned to the bench where Phil was waiting.

"Well," I asked. "Did you pick a name?"

"Actually, I did." Phil seemed surprised at himself. "As I prayed, I realized I really like the name, Alex." I laughed in relief.

"That's exactly the name I want too! The baby book says it means *helper of mankind.* Alex is the perfect name for our son." We agreed to use my father's name, Paul, as the middle name, so a few moments later when Jane arrived, we were ready.

The elevator buttons blinked slowly as we rode up to the nursery and then we stepped off the elevator into a sea of people. Apparently, the maternity floor was a very busy place. A gentleman approached Jane and identified himself as Mr. Clifton, the hospital administrator. Mr. Clifton directed us to a small room with a large window that looked out at the nursing station. As we were seated, I noticed nurses and aides stealing glances at us through the window.

"I hope it is acceptable," Mr. Clifton said. "But a few of our senior staff would like to be present when we bring the baby in." He didn't wait for a response but hurried off to tell everyone we had arrived. Phil and I looked at each other in confusion. We had chosen to come to the hospital on our own, so we could meet our new son and have some time alone before we introduced him to family and friends. Now it seemed our first meeting was going to be the morning's entertainment for some strangers. But we didn't feel confident enough to ask for privacy, so when the nurse finally wheeled in the portable crib, the room was crowded with people, watching our every expression. But at that moment, it seemed like it was just the three of us. The sides of the crib were clear, and I caught my first glimpse of our baby. We had been told that he was over nine pounds, but he seemed incredibly small, especially when the nurse lifted him from the bed and held him out to me.

"Mr. and Mrs. Migit, I would like you to meet your son." I carefully took Alex in my arms and watched him, transfixed. Our son. I smiled down at the face I had seen for the past year; this was the little boy who had floated in my dreams.

"Hello, Alex," I whispered. Then I spoke the words I had waited a lifetime to say. "I am your mother." Next to me I sensed Phil shift closer and I smiled up at him.

"I told you he was beautiful." Phil nodded, but seemed unable to talk, and hearing small sniffles from across the room, I suddenly remembered we had an audience.

The nurse said, "Mrs. Migit, the clothes the baby is wearing need to stay here, so we would like you to change him into the clothing you brought." Looking around the room I realized that these people were going to watch me as I changed my baby's clothes for the first time. I carefully laid him on the table, but the height was awkward, and I felt like I was all thumbs. The room remained silent as I changed Alex into the tuxedo sleeper I had bought last summer during one of my undercover shopping trips. Next, another nurse sat beside us and began to explain Alex's feeding and sleeping schedule. She spoke so fast I was in a panic that I would never remember half of what she said. Another nurse noticed my confusion, and she took pity on me.

"It's okay, Mommy," she said, handing me a stack of information. "It's all written here for you. You'll do just fine." More people entered the room, and I saw they were all carrying supplies: diapers, bottles, and even a case of formula. Within minutes, Phil was loaded down and on his way to get the car. Carefully placing Alex in the car seat we had brought, I turned to Jane. Our small audience had disappeared and we stood alone in the corridor.

"I'll meet you at the courthouse tomorrow," she said as she zipped her briefcase.

"We will go before the judge and he will grant temporary custody of the baby until we can get the home study finished." She smiled as she touched Alex's thick black hair. "Congratulations, you have a beautiful son." Suddenly, I was standing alone, holding the car seat, wondering where Phil would meet us. I looked down at my sleeping baby and felt a rush of wonder. We were going to take our baby home.

Our hands shook as Phil and I struggled to fasten the

car seat in the back of our station wagon. Checking the strap several times, Phil finally approved the fit and then we pulled out of the parking lot. My husband, who had always dreamed of being a race car driver, was driving so slowly other cars were passing us. Turning in my seat, I barely blinked as I watched our baby sleep through it all. It seemed impossible that barely an hour ago we had traveled this same road, just the two of us. And now there were three; a family.

As we approached our neighborhood, we saw the elementary school had a number of cars in the lot, and we noticed the American flags out front. Suddenly, I remembered that it was election day. Phil maneuvered into a parking place and we discussed how we should proceed. "He's sleeping so well, and I really don't want to take him in with a group of people." I made my first motherly decision. "You go vote and I'll stay here; when you come back, I can vote." Phil nodded and headed for the school. I continued to stare at Alex, wanting so badly to take him out of the seat and hold him. He seemed so tiny. His dark hair fell in soft waves over his forehead, and I was struck by how beautiful he was. I contented myself with stroking his velvety hand as I waited for Phil to come back.

As Phil opened the car door, Alex made a soft sound and moved around restlessly. We both held our breath as we waited to see if he would wake, but a moment later he settled down to sleep again. I made myself climb out of the car, reluctant to be separated for even a moment. But

Phil and I had voted in every Presidential election since we were eighteen, and we were determined to keep our record.

"Do you think he might wake up while you are gone?" Phil whispered. "What should I do if he cries?"

I reassured him, "He seems pretty content. I don't think he will wake up." Phil looked doubtful.

"Hey, do me a favor, will you?" He asked as I started to shut the door.

"Sure. What?"

"Vote a straight ticket."

Chapter Twenty

Our first night together was busy as Alex was welcomed into our family. My parents, Paul and Roberta Campbell, were the first to arrive, and I was thrilled to present our new son. We had decided to give Alex the middle name of Paul, to honor my dad, and I prayed that Alex would grow into a man of God, just like his namesake. My mom swaddled her newest grandchild and settled into the big rocking chair to bond. Soon, Phil's folks, Ed and Orva Migit, entered the family room, along with Phil's brother, Glen, and his son Matthew. I smiled as I saw my mom gently hand Alex over to his other Grandma. Blinking away the tears, I realized just how much love this tiny baby would receive.

My cousin, Brenda, and Phil's sister, Kim, were next to arrive, carrying armloads of gifts, and the family room began to look like a toy store with boxes scattered everywhere. Soon, my younger brother, Scott, and his family joined us. His wife Yvette, was pregnant, and as she held Alex, she spoke softly to their four year old daughter, "See Annie, in a few months we will have a baby boy, just like Alex."

My twin brother, Dave, lived in Minnesota with his wife Kathy, and daughters Erin and Shauna. He called to say they would visit just as soon as the girls had a break at school. Phil's sister Val called from Tulsa, where her husband Tom attended Oral Roberts University. Their son Michael was almost two years old, and Val was expecting their second child. In fact, she was due the same week as Yvette; in just a few months, Alex would have two more cousins to grow up with.

We had decided to make our first night a family affair, but I knew tomorrow would be just as busy with friends who were anxious to meet our son. Alex slept through most of the excitement, and by the time our last visitor left that evening, we were exhausted, but too excited to rest. Phil and I spent precious time cuddling our baby and letting him learn our voices. "He is beautiful, isn't he?" I echoed the words that had been spoken all evening. I knew every mother thought her baby was beautiful, but I was convinced that Alex had something special. His dark hair was thick and full and he had the longest eyelashes I had ever seen on a baby. His brown eyes sparkled as he seemed to study our faces intently. I watched as Phil held our son and stroked his soft cheek. It seemed that all of the tension and fear of the past few weeks had finally melted away and my husband's face was filled with wonder at the precious gift we had been given.

After a moment, Phil turned to me and said, simply,

"Thank you." I laid my head on his shoulder and we sat for a long time like that; finally a family.

Later I settled Alex in his new crib and lay down on the daybed we had put in the nursery. It seemed like I had just drifted off when I heard a small whimper. I was up and across the room in a flash. Alex regarded me solemnly—his only sound was that first small noise that had woken me. I gingerly gathered him up and went to the kitchen to prepare the bottle. A glance at the clock revealed the time as 2 a.m. He had slept for about four hours. I laid Alex in his cradle as I warmed the bottle and held my breath, waiting for him to cry again. But he seemed content to wait for his dinner and snuggled down to take the bottle as soon as I offered it to him. Settling into the rocking chair, I enjoyed my first private time with my baby. The rush of the day gave way to a deep peace as I stroked his tiny fist.

My son. Memories flashed of that Christmas Eve promise almost two years earlier. Although each day since had seemed like a lifetime, now I was overcome with gratitude. God was so faithful. The journey had seemed impossible at times, but the reward was beyond my dreams. God had gifted us with this beautiful child to love and raise for His glory. I thought of the other promise I had received. Alex had been born in November. God had promised us a son in May of next year. For a moment, I struggled with confusion as I wondered how that child would come. But God's peace quickly settled over me as I heard Him whisper, *Trust Me.* I gazed down at my now sleeping baby, and I was content to trust again.

Eight in the morning found Phil kneeling beside the daybed, watching me sleep. I had repeated the feeding process at 6 a.m. and was enjoying my rest.

Phil nudged me awake with the reminder, "Hey, we have to be in court at nine." Alex barely woke as I dressed him in his new, blue suit that had been a gift from Kim. A few minutes later, Phil and I retraced our route from yesterday, and I was again struck by how quickly things could change. Arriving at the courthouse with little time to spare, we were met by Jane.

"Let's step in here while we wait our turn," Jane said as she ushered us into a conference room. I caught a glimpse of the carved oak door across the hall, where family court was conducted.

Jane smiled down at Alex and asked, "How was your night?"

"Great!" Phil replied. I raised my eyebrow at him; he had slept through all the feedings, but I smiled and nodded my agreement.

"He was perfect." I carefully took Alex from the car seat and handed him to Jane, who was wearing a look that said, "Please let me hold him". Alex chose that moment to wake and Jane smiled at his solemn appraisal.

"He really is a beautiful baby." Jane looked at me and continued, "Right now Holly is meeting with the judge. When she is finished and has left the courthouse, we will be taken into the courtroom and the judge will ask you a few questions." Jane must have noticed my alarmed expression because she quickly continued, "Don't worry, it's routine. As long as he is satisfied with Holly's answers, everything should be fine." Jane glanced down at Alex again, and I sensed she was avoiding my gaze.

"What kind of questions?" Phil asked.

"Well, he wants to know if you can support Alex financially, and if you are committed to being his parents always, that kind of thing." Jane's voice trailed off as she saw Phil shake his head.

"I know what he will ask us," Phil said quietly. "But what is he asking Holly right now?"

"Oh." Jane handed Alex back to me and turned to gather up some papers that were lying on the table. "He just wants to know if she is placing Alex for adoption of her own free will, without coercion. And he will ask if she will be receiving any financial recompense from you. And if she is sure this is the decision she wants to make, that kind of thing." Jane pointed to some papers and held out a pen to Phil.

"I just need your signature on these, please." Phil sat down to read the papers and I stepped closer to Jane

"Everything is going to work out, though, right? I mean, Holly already signed the forms yesterday relinquishing her rights. She can't change her mind now; isn't that true?"

Jane continued to avoid my gaze as she answered.

"There's nothing to worry about. Now, Debbi, you sign

after Phil, and I will witness the signatures, and we will be ready when they call us." With shaking hands, I signed the papers that would give us temporary custody of Alex. Jane explained that after the adoption became final, we would receive a new birth certificate that named us as Alex's parents, just as if we had given birth to him. A moment later a knock sounded on the door, and the court clerk looked in.

"Ms. Connors, could I speak to you for a moment?" Jane frowned and quickly left the room as I gathered Alex tighter in my arms. Phil came to stand beside us, and I watched as he gently smoothed our son's cheek. I read in my husband's eyes the same concern I felt. *What if Holly changed her mind at the last minute?* In spite of Jane's assurances, I knew that the law still held a few loopholes. If the judge was not satisfied with Holly's responses to his questions, he could set aside her signed declaration that vacated her rights to Alex. *And what if the judge decided we were not the appropriate parents for Alex? What if he did not agree with transracial adoptions and decided to place Alex in foster care until an African American or Native American family was selected?.* I began to shake as I realized there was a possibility that we could walk out of the courthouse today without Alex. But surely God had not brought us this far just to take our son away.

"It's okay," Phil whispered. I reached for his hand and let my husband's faith settle me as he repeated, "God is in this. It will be okay." The door swung open and Jane bustled in, smiling.

"It's our turn," she said. "Holly gave the answers the judge needed to hear, and she has left the courthouse. Judge Ransom wants to speak with you now." I sank against Phil in relief and met his eyes. Now there was just one more hurdle to clear. I cuddled Alex in my arms as we entered the courtroom. Judge Ransom was seated behind a large desk that stood on a raised dais. The court reporter sat nearby with her fingers poised over the machine. Jane ushered us up to the front of the room where we stood to be addressed by the judge.

"Good morning," Judge Ransom smiled down at Alex. "What a beautiful baby!" I resisted nudging Phil.

"Thank you—" My mind went blank. *What was I supposed to call him? Sir? Your Honor? Judge Ransom? I glanced at his name plate. Tom?*

Phil's deep voice sounded behind me, "Thank you, Your Honor, we think so too." Thankful for Phil's self-confidence, I listened as he answered most of the judge's questions; I was surprised that the interview was over in less than ten minutes.

"I must say, I am very impressed with this case," Judge Ransom said as he studied our file. "First, the young woman I spoke with earlier is thoughtful and mature. I believe she has given this adoption plan much thought and she is especially at peace with you as the adoptive parents. I have also read the report from your attorney, and I believe that you are ideally suited to be Alex's parents. Transracial adoption is not an easy course, but I believe you have the resources and support to make a wonderful life for this child. I am granting your petition for adoption." I realized I had been holding my breath as the judge spoke, and now I felt a surge of excitement. It was really happening. Alex was truly going to be ours! Amid congratulations from the judge and clerks, we made our way to the door of the courtroom, then Judge Ransom spoke again. "There is just one thing—" My heart dropped as I turned to face him. *Judge Ransom had just granted our petition. He certainly wouldn't change his mind now!*

The judge continued.

"This will be my last family court proceeding; after today I am moving to criminal court. I am happy to end my time as a family court judge with your case, and I wonder if you would grant me a special privilege?" We nodded and even Jane and the court attendants seemed surprised. Judge Ransom took out a large calendar and began to flip through the pages.

"As we have explained, the home study will have to be completed and then you will be seen by another judge who will grant permanent custody of your son. Normally we leave the scheduling up to the lawyers and case workers, but if you would indulge me, I would like the privilege of deciding your final adoption date." The judge glanced at the calendar and then seemed to look right at me as he announced. "On May 19th, 1989, Alex will legally be your son, forever."

The voices around me seemed to fade as I remembered

another Judge's decree, given to me just a few months earlier.

On May 19, 1989, you will embrace your son.

"See, I told you it was going to be okay." Phil glanced at me as we drove away from the courthouse, but his triumphant words trailed off as he noticed my silent tears. "Hey," he said gently. "Are you okay? I know it was stressful, but it's done now." When I didn't respond he quickly pulled into a parking lot and turned to face me. "We just have to go through the home study and in six months it will be final. Six months will fly by, you'll see."

Shaking my head I explained, "No, that's not it. I was thinking about what the judge said about the date that Alex will legally be our son." As the reality of what had just happened continued to sink in, my voice broke as I faced my husband to share our miracle.

"Phil, I have something to tell you."

Chapter Twenty-One

MAY 1990

The ringing of the phone startled Alex and he quickly turned his head, smearing mashed bananas across his cheek. Grabbing a napkin, I wiped his face as I grabbed for the phone. Motherhood was teaching me all kinds of new skills, and I was becoming a master of multi-tasking.

"Hello?" I reached into the cabinet behind me and grabbed a teething cookie, which caused Alex to squeal with delight.

"Debbi?" The serious tone of Janice's voice removed my smile, and I settled into the kitchen chair to hear her out.

"Please pray, right now!" Janice's voice was shaking. "My niece, Michelle, just called and she is on her way to the Planned Parenthood clinic to have an abortion. She didn't even tell me she was pregnant, probably because she knew I would counsel her against abortion. I asked her to come over here and talk to me first, but she says her mind is made up. I don't have a car today, and she is in the waiting room right now—I wouldn't be able to get there in time anyway. So now, all we can do is pray." Janice began to cry as I prayed for God to protect Michelle's unborn baby.

After a few moments, we ended the call, and I lifted Alex from his high chair to hold him close. It was moments like these that made me so grateful all over again that Holly had decided against abortion. I snuggled my son and carried him to the family room so he could play and I could pray.

"Mama?" Alex touched my cheek where the tears had started to fall. At eighteen months he was a bundle of energy most of the time, but he also seemed unusually sensitive to other people's moods. I quickly wiped the tears and picked up a ball to roll back and forth. It seemed that in the past few moments, the burden had lifted and I knew it was time to release Michelle to God's hands. Nap time came soon after, and I had just pulled Alex's door closed when the phone rang again. Janice's voice was still tearful, but I soon learned they were tears of joy.

"Debbi, Michelle changed her mind! She said that just before they were about to call her name, she suddenly knew there had to be another way. She is coming over here right now and she asked me to call you. She wants to plan for adoption." My breath caught as I thought about the possibility of another baby so soon. But before that idea had a chance to take root, the Lord spoke clearly to me.

"This child is for someone else." I felt a quick stab of loss, but pushed it away. I had learned that God's way was better than mine; our family would grow again in His time.

After promising Janice I would call her back, I hung up and dialed another number.

"Nancy, are Tony and Mary still in the States?" Nancy and her husband Bruce were our pastors and recently they had introduced us to their friends, Tony and Mary, who were missionaries to Mexico. Tony and Mary were home on furlough, but were scheduled to return to the field any day. When we met, Mary had quizzed me about adoption; she and Tony had been married for seven years and had no children. Now, I wondered if this was God's answer to their desire for a child. Nancy quickly gave me the number where Mary could be reached, and I made the call. My heart pounded as I thought of the possibilities for blessing or pain. *What if Michelle changed her mind again? What if Michelle was willing, but Tony and Mary felt differently. What if—?*

"Mary, this is Debbi Migit. I'd like to talk to you about a situation—"

A few days later I had the privilege of introducing Tony and Mary to Michelle. As they sat together in my living room and discussed the terms of their adoption plan, I caught a glimpse of the future God had for my life. I knew that someday, in some way, I would be involved in an adoption ministry. The whispers of God that came to me in my quiet times told me that He was laying a foundation for something wonderful to come. But even though I waited expectantly for God's direction for ministry, my heart still longed for more children to call our own.

Chapter Twenty-Two

CHRISTMAS 1998

Snuggling in my chair, I watched as Phil and Alex wound the Christmas lights around the tree. Alex had fixed me a cup of cocoa, and I sipped it as I studied my husband and son. It seemed impossible that ten years had passed so quickly. Our beautiful baby had grown into a young boy, and I knew that it was just a matter of time before he was taller than I. His dark hair and eyes gave him a serious look, but that was often erased when he smiled and one dimple peeked out. He was already showing the signs of an athlete and was especially gifted in running. Art was another favorite occupation, and I was amazed at the intricate designs and details he gave to his drawings.

Alex carefully hung the last ornament, and then turned to bring me the Christmas stockings. As usual, he carried not only stockings for the three of us, but an extra one, too. As he had explained when he was four years old, when he had added the extra stocking for the first time, it was for the baby brother who was coming some day. I smiled as I reached for them and then saw that he held a smaller stocking that he had found in the box of decorations.

At my questioning look, Alex solemnly said, "There will be a girl, too." I caught Phil's look and realized he had heard the declaration. Although our days were filled with love, a new restlessness was developing in me. Alex was ten years old now. I was longing for more children and becoming concerned that it might never happen again. There had been several other opportunities to adopt, but each time it seemed God had said, "*not yet.*" Phil and I were in our forties now; time was at a premium.

Later that night I watched the lights flicker on the tree and thought of that Christmas twelve years ago, when I had received the letter from Vicki. So much had happened since then. I wondered why my faith was so low at this point, when I had seen so many wonderful miracles already. I was beginning to feel a certain kinship with the children of Israel.

Now, as I looked at the five stockings that hung by our tree, I wondered if God was trying to prepare me through Alex's words; a boy and a girl. I looked around our home and had a sense of deja vu. While our little house on Bittersweet Lane was perfect for the three of us, it would be very crowded if we added even one more child. Excitement fluttered inside me as I thought about the possibilities. It occurred to me that God might just follow the same plan He had before Alex was born. If He was indeed going to increase our family, maybe it was time to move again. And I knew just the house.

Soon after Phil and I were married, we had been invited

to visit the home of our pastors, Jim and Nancy. They had just finished building their new house, and after dinner, they offered to give us a tour. The brick ranch sat on an acre of ground, surrounded by spruce trees. The house was large and comfortable for their family of five children. As we enjoyed our dessert that afternoon, I had gazed out the picture window in the family room, watching as a deer drank from the creek in the back. Sudden longing caused me to whisper, "*God, could we live here someday?*"

Years later, Jim and Nancy's daughter, Christine, had become one of my closest friends, and I had shared my dream with her. Jim and Nancy had sold the house years earlier, but now it was on the market again. As an added bonus, I had recently discovered that the house was right down the lane from one of Alex's closest friends. The brick ranch would be a perfect place to raise our three children. All we had to do was sell our home, buy the ranch, and wait for the babies to arrive. I smiled at my own naiveté. If experience had taught me anything, it was that things didn't always go quite the way we thought they should.

Now as I watched Alex subtly shaking a Christmas package hidden under the tree, I was reminded that God's ways were infinitely better than mine. Smoothing my hand over the small, velvet stockings, I pondered that maybe God was reviving several dreams. It was time to let my faith be stirred again.

Chapter Twenty-Three

April 1999

"Debbi, are you still interested in adopting again?" Christine watched as Alex and her son, Nic, played Frisbee. We often met at the park to visit, and let our boys run off some energy. Now I faced my friend and felt my breath catch in my throat. I knew that Christine would not ask that question lightly. Christine and her husband, Keith, had been through the adoption process twice in the past year. It had been fascinating to watch how God had led them each step of the way. In the beginning, they had planned to adopt a baby girl from China. But after several months of obstacles, they had started to wonder if that was really God's direction for them.

So, one evening, Phil and I had joined Keith and Christine at a meeting sponsored by a brand new adoption agency in our city. Although Phil and I sensed this was not our avenue for more children, Keith and Christine were quickly matched with a birthmother, Mandi, who was carrying a biracial baby. I had shared Christine's excitement as she prepared for the birth, and was with her on the morning when she received the long awaited call from the adoption agency. But our excitement quickly turned to tears as the heartbreaking news came. Mandi had delivered a baby boy three days earlier, but had changed her mind about the adoption. She was keeping the baby.

The summer passed as Keith and Christine continued to try to adopt from China. They were encouraged by a dream that Christine's sister, Julie, had received. In the dream, Julie met a young woman who was pregnant. Julie was told that Christine's baby would be a girl, and was coming from a place that started with the letter "C". She was also told a specific month and day in July, and finally, the month, 'February'.

One day, Christine had received a call from Tina, a woman who was also on the waiting list for China. "I remembered your name from one of our adoption meetings, and I thought I would give you a call. Could I ask how things are going with your adoption?" Tina seemed as discouraged as Christine felt. As they spoke, Tina casually mentioned the name of an agency in Chicago.

"We are planning to contact them; they place only African American and biracial infants." That night Keith and Christine discussed the phone call.

"Let's call that agency that Tina mentioned," Christine said. "They are only three hours away. That's a lot closer than China!" Within a few weeks, their files had been transferred and they were on a new waiting list. But a week later, they were shocked to receive a phone call from the new agency.

"We have a waiting child, if you are interested."

"But, you said the wait would be about a year—are you sure you meant to call us—we've only been on the list for a week!" Christine answered.

"This is a special circumstance." Megan, the case-worker, seemed to hesitate. "Matthew is six months old, and his birthmother brought him to us earlier this week. He has just tested positive for HIV. You were one of the few couples that had indicated you were willing to take an HIV baby, so we wanted to contact you about Matthew." Keith and Christine quickly made plans to travel the following day to pick up Matthew.

Late that night the phone rang, again.

"Christine, I'm so sorry to tell you this. Matthew isn't available after all. I know this is devastating for you, but I want you to know that we are moving you to the top of our list. The next baby that is born will be yours." Christine and I had cried together, again.

"I don't understand!" I wasn't sure which of us said it first. I had to believe there was a reason for these disappointments, and I tried to encourage my friend that in the end, God would bring just the right child to them. But even as they anticipated another call from the agency, their faith was stretched to the limit. Finally, one winter morning, Christine called me. "We have a baby girl!" I was excited, but also very concerned; I wasn't sure if they could take one more heartbreak.

Five days later I saw Mariah for the first time. Her

beautiful brown eyes captured me, and I had a hard time handing her back to her new mommy. Together, Christine and I marveled at how accurate Julie's dream had been. Mariah came from Chicago, and she was born in February. But the most amazing thing was when we remembered the specific date that had been given to Julie in the dream. It was exactly nine months before Mariah's birth date. Julie had even been told Mariah's date of conception!

Keith and Christine's three teen-age children were eager to help out with the care of their new sister, and I left their home that day rejoicing in God's faithfulness. But my heart longed even more for another child. One morning, about two months later, I received another phone call from Christine.

"Debbi, do you remember Mandi?" I could tell from the excitement in her voice that this was good news.

"Of course. Don't tell me she has decided after a full year that she wants you to adopt the baby after all?" I said in disbelief.

"No! She is pregnant and about to deliver another baby boy. She says that this time she knows adoption is the right decision." I rejoiced with my friend, even as I prayed that there would be no more heartbreak. A few weeks later Christine and Keith added another new baby, Jonathan, to their family.

Now, as I cuddled Mariah, and Christine fed Jonathan, I considered Christine's question. *Was I interested in adopting again?* I had watched the process Keith and Christine had gone through in the past two years. I knew that adoption was a blessing; but it was also an emotional roller coaster at times. *Was I ready for that?*

Christine must have read my thoughts.

"I can see now that if we had adopted Mandi's first baby, we wouldn't have been able to get Mariah. But God is so good, and He brought Jonathan to us too. It was so hard to go through at the time, but I don't regret a thing now." Christine continued, "There is a young woman at our church who is pregnant and she would like to meet with you and Phil to discuss adopting the baby."

"Do you know when the baby is due?" I asked.

"Early October, I think. She asked me a lot of questions about you and Phil and Alex, and she seemed happy with my answers, because she asked me to set up a meeting if you are interested. What should I tell her?"

As I drove home, I thought about my answer to Christine. *Yes* seemed so tame for what I was feeling. Pulling into the driveway of our home on Bittersweet Lane, I studied the *For Sale* sign that was displayed in the front yard, and I again marveled at the timing of God. If we sold the house soon, we could be moved in and be ready when the new baby arrived in October.

Preparing dinner that evening, it was difficult to keep my excitement from Alex, but I hesitated to get his hopes up. He had waited patiently for his baby brother, and there had been a few disappointments along the way. There would be plenty of time to prepare him later. That evening when Phil and I were finally alone, I shared the news with him.

"The birthmother's name is Ashley, and she would like to meet with our attorney to set up all of the legal paperwork as soon as possible. Assuming we say yes, of course."

I was practically jumping up and down in my excitement. I hadn't realized how much I had missed out on sharing the anticipation of Alex's birth. I was determined to enjoy the preparation time for this baby.

Ten years of fatherhood had mellowed Phil a great deal. I could see my excitement reflected in his eyes as we stayed up late that night, planning our future.

The next weeks were busy as we scheduled appointments, first with Ashley and then with our attorney. My experience with other birthmothers in the past few years had prepared me a little, but it was still unnerving to meet the young woman who was carrying our child. My heart broke for her, even as I rejoiced for us.

Still, I was unprepared when during one of our conversations, Ashley said, "I would like for you to be in the delivery room with me."

Joy and terror seemed to mix equally in my heart. While I knew my bond with Alex was as deep as any mother's, I still remembered those three long days when he was in the hospital nursery, and I was kept from him. To be able to hold this baby from birth would be a rare gift, and I expressed my gratitude to Ashley.

In the years since Alex's adoption, some of our state

laws had been revised, and now Phil and I were required to have our home study finished before the baby could be placed with us. Although the paperwork would be done much closer to the birth, we were advised to have our fingerprints and background check done as quickly as possible, since that could take several months to complete. After that, all we had to do was wait.

Spring rushed by as we finished the requirements and continued to talk with Ashley by phone, since she had moved to another state to live with some friends. She planned to return to our state a few weeks before the baby was due, and she would stay with Christine and her family while we waited for the baby to be born. Everything seemed to be working out smoothly, so I wasn't surprised when, one day in June, we experienced another victory. Our house had sold.

Chapter Twenty-Four

June 1999

"Just sign right here, and I can deliver the contract to the buyers on my way home." Sandy Glover had been our realtor for the past several months, and I sensed she was almost as relieved as we were to sell our house. Still, it was truly a bittersweet moment as I signed the paper that would move us from our home on Bittersweet Lane.

Although I was excited to move, I was disappointed that we hadn't been able to purchase the brick ranch I dreamed about. Christine's folks had sold it several years earlier to a doctor and his family. That family had since built a new home just down the road, and had sold the brick ranch several weeks earlier. When we learned that it was no longer available, I had spent days on end, touring homes in the area until we found one we felt we could call home. I tried to content myself with the thought that God had provided a lovely home in its place.

As soon as Sandy left, Phil picked up the phone to contact the family who owned the house we would be purchasing. I was relieved that we had found the house, since the offer we had just accepted required us to move within six weeks. I looked around the living room and mentally began packing as Phil finished his conversation. When he returned to the living room, I immediately realized he had bad news.

"They changed their minds." Phil sat next to me on the sofa and I watched to see if he was joking. He realized what I was doing and hastened to assure me, "No, I'm not kidding. They just made the decision today. They don't want to sell their house after all. They were going to call us tonight, so they were a little shocked when I told them we just accepted a binding offer on our house. They apologized, of course, especially since we have been planning this for the past two months. But apparently, their kids really don't want to move and they finally realized how upset they are."

"So what you are telling me is that in six weeks we are—"

"Homeless. Yep, that pretty much sums it up." Phil shook his head as if he didn't know whether to laugh or not. Seeing the stricken look on my face made the decision for him.

"Hey, c'mon. It will be okay." He pulled me close. "You love to go house hunting, remember?"

"Sure, as long as I know I still have a house to come home to! What about Alex? We were finally going to be in the school district we wanted for him. And he was so excited about that house. It had a great yard, and kids his age and—" my voice trailed off as I remembered Phil and Alex's favorite part of the house.

"I'm sorry about your hot tub." I touched Phil's arm but he shrugged.

"No big deal," he said. "There's a lot of upkeep on those things anyway. It will just be one less thing to worry about. Right now we just have to focus on finding a house for the three of us to live in."

"Four of us," I reminded him as I rummaged through the drawer that held the magazine with the latest real estate listings. I pushed down the panic that threatened to overwhelm me. I couldn't spend time looking for houses; I had to pack and move in six weeks, and then prepare for the baby that was coming in a few more months. Doubt filled my heart as I flipped through the pages of pictures. *What on earth was God doing? Didn't He realize how long it had taken us to finally decide on the house on Hickory Grove?* I had visited every house in our school district and there was not one other possibility.

I thought again about the brick ranch that Christine's parents had built—my dream house. It wasn't available anymore, but maybe there was something else in that area for sale. Alex's friend Tyler lived close by, and I was friends with his mom, Tracy. I decided that networking was our best resource, and Tracy seemed like the logical place to start.

I picked up the phone and dialed Tracy's number. After quickly explaining the situation to my friend, I asked if there were any other houses for sale near them. I was surprised by her chuckle.

"Maybe I didn't make the problem clear," I said, a little annoyed. "Homeless; in six weeks."

"Oh honey, I'm not laughing at you, I'm laughing with you," she said. "It's just that this is so *you!* I was going to wait to call you tomorrow, but apparently God couldn't wait for this little surprise."

"Tracy." Annoyance warred with a smidgeon of hope.

"Debbi, I just came home from a neighborhood barbeque. You remember the big brick ranch you love so much?" *Remember? I immediately saw myself sitting in the living room of the house, whispering, "God, could I live here someday?"*

"Of course," I answered. "What about it? You told me it sold two months ago."

"Well, it did, but it didn't. I just spoke with the owners at the party tonight, and they cancelled the contract with the buyers. I guess the financing didn't work out. They said the house is going on the market next week, so I'd call them right away and you might even get it directly from them. They have already moved into their new home, so they are very motivated to sell. When I told them about you, they asked me to let you know it was back on the market. And by the way, they have done some updates since you were in it all those years ago. They even added a hot tub on the back patio. Welcome to the neighborhood!"

A few moments later I hung up the phone and slowly

walked to the rocking chair. As I sank into the cushion I began to cry, not just because I knew we were going to buy the house of my dreams. I was simply overwhelmed by God's love. He had heard the whispered prayer of a young bride all those years ago, and He remembered. I let the knowledge of His faithfulness soak deep into my spirit, never realizing how much my faith would be tested in the coming months.

Chapter Twenty-Five

AUGUST 1999

"Alex, would you bring in some more ice from the freezer, please?" I put down the silver tray I was holding and reached for more vegetables from the refrigerator. From the back of the house, I could hear the hum of the hot tub, mingled with the laughter of dozens of family and friends who had come to *warm* our new home. I took a moment to savor the feeling of joy. We had moved into the brick ranch the previous month, and we were all adjusting to our new home. First of all, it was almost three times the size of our little house on Bittersweet Lane. We were happy for the intercom system that made it easier to communicate, especially when Alex was in his downstairs 'apartment'. In the years since Christine's family had built the house, the trees had grown tall and lush, but the creek still bubbled at the back of our property. Each house in our neighborhood had at least an acre of ground, so I had asked Phil to hang a large triangle on the back patio, so I could call Alex home each evening. He and his friends often went exploring in the fields and woods surrounding us. We were far enough in the country for privacy, but still only three miles from our church and Alex's school. Our new baby was due to be born in six weeks. I had never been so content. *And yet*—

I quickly pushed the thought away and picked up a bowl of chips. As I mingled with our guests, I kept my concerns to myself. In the past few weeks, the phone calls with Ashley had seemed brief and strained. I glanced down the hall toward the bedroom we had designated as the nursery. We had recently been told that the baby Ashley was carrying was a girl, and I was anxious to begin decorating. Next, I wandered down the stairs to the lower level and headed toward the sounds of a ping pong game in the recreation room. I carefully opened the door, and then ducked as a white ball sailed by my head.

"Sorry, Mom," Alex grinned as he took the bowl of chips from me. "Nic is using too much English on his serve." The sound of the phone ringing in the distance interrupted any ping pong instruction I was going to offer to Nic, and a moment later I heard my name being called from upstairs.

"Debbi, telephone." Standing at the bottom of the stairs, I asked Christine to take a message, but she shook her head and mouthed, "It's Ashley." I hurried upstairs to my bedroom and picked up the line on my table. My heart tattooed as I greeted Ashley, but somehow I already knew how this phone call would end.

Fifteen minutes later I rejoined the party. The hot tub still bubbled, and our guests continued to enjoy themselves. But for me, the party was over. There would be no baby. Ashley had changed her mind.

December 4, 1999

Snow smeared across the windshield as the wipers slashed back and forth. I drove the country road carefully since we often were the last to see a snowplow. I knew I should be relieved by the doctor's diagnosis, but it seemed that all I felt these days was numb.

A week after Ashley's phone call, I had become ill with pneumonia and it had taken several months to recover my strength. I knew that part of the problem was grief, which had continued through Thanksgiving; it was just now starting to lift. We had closed up the nursery the day after the house warming party, and I hadn't even gone back in that room since that night. It hurt too much. Now as I drove along I had the doctor's release to begin my life again. I just wasn't sure where to start.

"Will you open your heart to adoption again?" I swerved the car as those startling words penetrated my heart. I recognized that still, small voice.

"No, God, I can't!" All of the pain of the past few months surfaced and I pulled off the road to cry. "It just hurts too much. I can't do it again." I didn't say the other words that I felt. *God, You hurt me. You set me up and then You let me down.* I knew that wasn't true, but I couldn't deny the emotions any longer and I poured out my hurt and frustration.

Snow had accumulated on the windshield by the time I was finished, and I realized I needed to hurry home before Phil and Alex began to worry. As I pulled onto the road, I felt something stirring that had been buried for a long time. Faith began to fill my heart again, and I realized I had given my answer without saying a word.

"*Will you open your heart to adoption again?*"

"Yes."

December 6, 1999

3:00 a.m.

I sat straight up in bed and looked around the darkened room. Although I was calm, I knew that something had wakened me, and I waited in the stillness.

A moment later I heard the words repeated, "*Your time as a family of three is almost over. You are about to become a family of four.*" For a moment I sat, smiling in the darkness, and then I laid back down next to Phil, who was sleeping soundly. And I slept again.

9:00 A.M.

The ringing phone interrupted my thoughts of the previous nights' encounter. I had been meditating on what

God meant when He said, "about to become." I knew from experience that His timing was often different from mine, and I was trying to prepare my heart to be patient. The phone continued to ring and finally I reached over to answer it.

"Debbi, it's Christine." My friend sounded different from her usual bubbly self. She had taken it hard when the adoption with Ashley had fallen through. I was happy Christine had called, because I wanted to share with her the message I had received in the night. But before I could tell her about it, she rushed on.

"Debbi, last night we received a phone call from our adoption agency that gave us Mariah. Her birthmother is pregnant again, and they asked us if we would adopt that baby, too. The birthmother wants the children to grow up together. But with Mariah and Jonathan just turning two, and having three teen-agers, Keith and I just know this isn't the right time for us to adopt again. But when I told them about you, the caseworker spoke to the birthmother and she has picked you and Phil; she wants you to adopt this baby, so Mariah can grow up knowing her sibling! Can you believe it?" My hand trembled as I tried to hold on to the phone. I suddenly knew the timing of *about to become.* It was now!

"Christine, are you sure?" I knew what it had cost her to make that decision. There had been other babies that Phil and I had said no to when we knew they weren't ours, but it still was a difficult and painful decision.

"Debbi, this is the right thing, I know it is. Mariah can grow up knowing her brother or sister, and Alex will finally have that sibling he has been waiting for. Debbi, I know this one is your baby!"

"Christine, I wanted to make sure how you felt before I told you what happened last night—" I shared with her the events of the past few days.

I could hear the tears in her voice as she said, "I have been praying every day for you to have another chance to adopt after Ashley changed her mind. It's amazing that God is using me and Keith to bring this baby to you and Phil. And now we won't just be friends, we'll be family!"

Christine quickly gave me the information to contact the agency, and less than an hour later, it was settled. When the baby was born in March, we would be the adoptive parents. That evening Phil and I explained to Alex that he truly was about to become a big brother. The next few weeks flew by with Christmas and New Years celebrations, and finally, on a cold day in early January, we met with the caseworker who would be completing our home study.

"It's really a blessing in disguise that you had that other adoption possibility this year." Erica Steller was friendly and efficient as she spent several hours helping us with our paperwork.

She didn't notice our confusion at her words, so Phil asked, "I'm not sure what you mean?"

"Oh, I'm sorry, I didn't mean to be insensitive about the other adoption that failed." Erica looked stricken. "What

I meant was, because of that possibility, you two already had your fingerprints and criminal background check all finished. And since it is good for a year, we can use it for this home study. If you hadn't had that done, I'd be worried that we wouldn't have the required paperwork ready in time for you to take this baby. But everything is in order now," she continued as she sealed the envelope with all of our information. "I will take this to the post office right now and send it off. I want it postmarked today, so you can receive your foster care license to adopt. I noticed that the baby is due on March second, which is your birthday, Debbi, right?" I smiled and nodded and Erica grinned back. "Well, happy birthday to you!" She stood and shook Alex's hand.

"Alex, you are going to be a wonderful big brother. I don't think I've ever known an eleven-year-old with your maturity. You are going to be a great help to your mom and dad." Erica bustled out the door and the three of us faced each other.

Memories of our time together flashed before me: the long bike rides that Phil and Alex took most week-ends, ending at the bottom of a steep hill, where I met them with the truck to save them the ride back up. Then we would head off to our favorite restaurant to try out the latest cuisine. Then there were Alex's marathon roller coaster rides with Phil and his quieter times with me, spent exploring the local antique stores. In just a few weeks, our lives together would change forever. And while I was thrilled, I was also a little melancholy. I wondered if this baby would be a boy or girl, and how Phil and I would adjust to having a newborn again. Phil was forty-seven, and I was about to be forty-five. I smiled again when I remembered the baby was due on my birth day. Although I knew due dates were often wrong, Alex had been born on his due date. Besides, I had been sharing my birth date with my twin brother all of my life; sharing it with my child could be fun too.

The next morning, Alex and I were starting out the door to go to the library when the phone rang. I ran back to grab it and was surprised to hear Erica's voice.

"Hello, Debbi, I have something to tell you." I gripped the phone and leaned against the counter. Trying to keep my face impassive for Alex's sake, I braced for bad news.

"I just received a phone call from the agency. I can't believe I'm about to say this, but congratulations, you have a healthy baby boy!" My expression must have alarmed Alex because he quickly came to my side.

"What is it?" he whispered. "Are you okay?" I nodded as I tried to take in the information Erica was sharing.

"The baby was born last night at around 11 p.m. The doctor had the due date wrong, so he is perfectly fine and is full–term. He will have to stay with a foster care family for a few days until his birthmother signs the papers to relinquish her rights. But as soon as that is done, you can come and get your son!" Erica gave a few more details, and then added, "By the way, I thought it was interesting that I had those papers postmarked last night. The agency director said that since the papers had already been sent they would follow through with the adoption. But if they had known the baby was going to be born so soon, they never would have been able to offer him to you because you wouldn't be able to get the license in time. But since it has been postmarked, the attorney has given the okay for you to have the baby. Isn't that amazing?"

I hung up the phone and looked at my son, Alex, my child of promise. Just a few miles away I had another son, waiting to come home. As I took in all of the facts Erica had just shared, I realized once again, just how precious God's timing was. He had chosen and handpicked these children to be ours. I put my arms around Alex and hugged him as I told him his prayers had finally been answered. He had a baby brother.

Chapter Twenty-Six

I snuggled Ethan Joseph in my arms as I sang the lullaby I hoped would settle him for the night. Phil and Alex were watching Phil's favorite Christmas movie, *It's a Wonderful Life*, at the other end of the living room. The tree sparkled in the darkened room, and I took a moment to reflect on the past year. Ethan was such a delight, even though his sleeping habits left something to be desired. It had been an adjustment for me to be up at all hours of the night with a newborn. Alex had been such an easy baby, that I wasn't prepared for Ethan's sleeping problems. In addition, Ethan had developed RSV when he was six weeks old and been hospitalized for three days. I was encouraged by remembering the name God had given us for him. Ethan meant strong, firm, and permanent. He had recovered and was a healthy little boy.

Since Ethan was fully African American, I had some new challenges in learning to care for his skin and hair. Christine had helped me with that, as she had been helped by other adoptive mothers. Although Ethan was not quite a year old, he and Alex were already inseparable. Alex had even requested that Ethan be given the same adoption date, and the judge had agreed. May 19th was a double celebration for us now.

I glanced down at my now sleeping son and smiled. Tomorrow would be our first Christmas together as a family of four. I looked over at the stockings that were hanging near the tree and was momentarily startled to see five stockings. Alex must have snuck the last one in after I put the others out.

I remembered several years ago when he had brought two extra stockings and said, "We are going to get a boy and a girl, mom." I snuggled Ethan closer and decided to hold on to my secret a little while longer. Alex was right. Our girl was coming soon.

Although I had received the dream several years earlier, the details were still vivid in my mind. I was standing in a large shopping center in the middle of a crowd of people. In the center was a man standing next to a round clothing rack that was filled with baby buntings. As the man held up a blue bunting he called the name of a couple, and they ran forward to take the garment from him. Everyone began to cheer and some even worshipped as the couple rejoiced. Somehow I knew that the bunting represented adoption and that each person who was called forward was going to adopt a baby. I heard the man call the name of some close friends, Dennis and Martha. A few years earlier, they had lost their nine-month-old baby boy, Joel, to a sudden case of meningitis. They had finally started to heal,

and I knew that recently they had been praying about adoption. In the dream, Dennis and Martha approached the man and were handed a blue bunting. I suddenly felt incredible joy and even a sense of healing from my own grief over the loss of Joel. Then the crowd parted and the man pointed to me, calling my name. I walked forward and with a smile he handed me a soft, pink bunting. The dream ended.

I had remembered the dream a few weeks later, when one day I felt directed to go into a clothing store. Trying to dismiss the feeling, I had argued that there was nothing there I needed since I had just explored the store the day before. I made it to my car before I finally gave in and returned to the store. And there, in the middle of the children's department, was a round rack with one lone, pink baby bunting, just like the one in my dream. I had purchased it and put it away for the day I would need it. The dream had taken on added significance a few months later, when Dennis and Martha announced their decision to travel to Russia to adopt their son, Victor.

Now, on Christmas Eve, I studied that small stocking my son had laid next to the hearth. I had recently received the answer to my question, "Father, when will our daughter come home?"

"February."

That was all I had heard, but it was enough to galvanize me as Christmas passed, and we entered the month of

January. In the past eighteen months we had moved into a new home, I had been very sick with pneumonia, and we had adopted a newborn baby. I never really had the time to unpack and settle into our home, so I asked my sister-in-law, Valerie, to come and help me out for a few days each week. She graciously agreed and we spent the month of January cleaning closets and organizing for my soon to be expanding family. However, I continued to keep that secret to myself.

Finally, on February first, the project was finished. Val left at 3 p.m. that day, and I looked around my newly organized home with a sense of satisfaction.

As I sat gazing out the picture window I spoke out loud, "Well, Lord, You said our daughter was coming in February. It's February 1st, so I'm ready when You are."

Five minutes later, the phone rang.

I looked at it for a moment and shook my head. *No, surely not.* It rang again, and I had a moment of fear that it would wake Ethan. I reached for the receiver with shaking hands, but by this time I wasn't really surprised when I heard Erica's voice on the other end.

"Debbi, how are you? How are Alex and Ethan?"

"Fine," I answered cautiously. "Is something wrong?"

"Actually, I think something might be very right." Erica said. "I just received a call from an agency in the southern part of the state. They have a newborn African American baby girl, just a few days old, but no waiting families at this time. They called us, and I immediately thought of you and Phil. Are you interested in adopting again?"

Moments later I called Phil to tell him we had a daughter.

"Let me think about it." Phil's response stunned me. Ethan's adoption had been so different from Alex's, and Phil loved being a dad to his two boys. We had certainly talked about adopting a baby girl soon, so I wasn't sure why he was so reluctant. My heart pounded as I considered the possibility that we might have to say no. I knew with all of my heart that this was our daughter. The agency wanted an answer by the following day, so there was no time for deep soul searching this time. I tried to stay calm as Phil and I agreed to talk and pray when he came home that night. After hanging up the phone, I began to pace the room in frustration. Erica had said that if we decided to adopt the baby, we could pick her up on Saturday, less than forty-eight hours from now. All I had were baby boy clothes, and it took every ounce of my self-control to keep from running out the door to the mall. My daughter was coming, and I didn't have a stitch of clothing for her! I kept busy with Ethan and managed to keep the secret from Alex when he came home from school. All the time I prayed that God would find a way to speak to Phil about this baby.

That evening, I had dinner waiting when Phil arrived with company. As soon as I saw John Eveans, my heart leaped with joy. Phil regarded me with a rueful grin.

"Look who showed up out of the blue." John had been Phil's friend even before we were married. John had a special gift of intercession and it seemed that we were one of his assignments. Although John lived almost an hour away, and we rarely saw him, he always managed to show up, unannounced, when we were facing a crisis. He usually came prepared with a word from the Lord for us, too. John gave me his famous bear hug.

"Hey, I hear you're about to be a mommy again!" I quickly looked at Phil and was thrilled to see him nodding. Later that evening, Phil related what had happened.

"Right after I hung up from talking to you, I took my Bible and went for a drive. I realized that there was one thing that I was concerned about the most, and it wasn't the cost." Phil gave a rueful grin and then continued.

"I'm not sure if I can explain this, but I'll try. My biggest fear is about raising a daughter. I have a clue about raising sons, but girls are a mystery to me." His look indicated that over the years I hadn't been much help in unraveling the mystery. "I know that girls receive a lot of their self-esteem from their relationship with their dad, and I just wasn't sure how good I'll be at that kind of thing." I didn't say anything, since I knew from experience that Phil was a little spare with compliments. I was curious to see what God had told him to change his mind. "Anyway, as I was praying about this, I happened to open my Bible and I read the first line of this verse in Song of Solomon, "*I am dark, but lovely*" (*Song of Solomon* 1:5, NKJV).

Phil's voice broke as he said, "As soon as I read that Scripture, I knew that our daughter will be the most beautiful girl in the world to me, and God will help me express that to her. Then when I got back to the shop, I saw John waiting in my office, and I knew what God had sent him to say, before he even opened his mouth. John said that he didn't know why he was there, but God had just told him to make the drive over and see what was going on with us; he would know what to do from there." Phil grinned. "As soon as I told John about your phone call, he got excited and said, "So that's what it is, congratulations on your new baby girl!" Phil and I laughed and cried together as we once again saw God's faithfulness in designing our family.

Later that night as everyone slept, I thought of the trip we would take the next day to bring our daughter home. I was excited and amazed at all that God had done; I was also a little worried about my ability to handle two babies at once. After Ethan was born, God had brought a wonderful friend and helper into our lives. Jenny attended Trinity, and she had been such a blessing in helping me care for Ethan. She and her sister Nora seemed like part of our family now. My mom also helped out as she was able. In addition, Christine's two daughters, Stephanie and Jennifer, often spent the night on our couch, ready to help with the night-time feedings. But ultimately, the responsibility of daily care rested with me, and I needed reassurance. Restlessly, I went into the living room and sought out my favorite spot to pray. Picking up my Bible, I began the conversation.

"Father, thank you so much for your faithfulness once again! You are amazing, God. If I wasn't living these experiences myself, I would have trouble believing they are really happening. But even in the middle of all these miracles, I still have doubts. How can that be, God? It's not you I doubt, it's me! Lord, I'm not sure if you remember, but my birthday is coming up in about a month, and I'm going to be forty- six years old. I'm concerned that I won't be able to give these children the kind of care they need. How can I do it, Lord? Alex is about to become a teen-ager, and Ethan just turned one; now we'll have a newborn. God, my heart is so delighted by the thought of my daughter. I just can't wait to see her. But Lord, please give me the reassurance that I need that I can be a good mother, even at my age." Tearfully I reached for my Bible and watched as the pages fluttered open to Isaiah. Then I read:

> "Even the youths shall faint and be weary, and the young men shall utterly fall, but those who wait on the Lord shall renew their strength. They shall mount up with wings like eagles, they shall run and not be weary; they shall walk and not faint."
> Isaiah 40:30–31 (NKJV)

Tears stained the pages as I once again witnessed God's faithfulness, even in the face of my unbelief. I was right;

this wasn't something I could do on my own. And thank God I didn't have to. I settled down to sleep. Tomorrow I would meet my daughter.

February 3, 2001

I gazed over at the silhouette of our sleeping baby girl. Even though she was less than a week old, I could already tell that she was going to be a true beauty. Stroking her tiny hand I looked up at Alex, who was riding in the front of the car beside his dad. It seemed like just a few moments ago that Alex had been the baby in the car seat, traveling to his new home. Now he was almost a teenager. Just a year earlier, we had made a similar trip to get Ethan. And as always, I was struck by the desire to suspend time, just so I could cherish this moment. My parents and Ethan were waiting for us at home, and experience had taught me that soon our home would be filled with family and friends, eager to meet our daughter.

"Katelynn."

I whispered the name and Phil asked, "Did you say something?"

"I think she is a Katelynn, not a Katherine," I responded. My conversation that afternoon with her birthmother teased my mind. We had spoken for just a few minutes, but I could tell that Natasha was at peace with her decision. I had assured her that in our home, birthmothers were spoken of with respect. We realized that they had made the most difficult, and courageous decision of their lives. Natasha had asked what we would name our daughter, and I had said we were considering Katherine. But now I knew it would be Katelynn, and we would call her Kate; the pure one. As we traveled home that night, I was aware of a deep settling in my spirit, and suddenly, I realized what it was. Contentment.

Chapter Twenty-Seven

APRIL 22, 2004

"The decorations are beautiful, Debbi. Did you do all this?" My friend, Connie, nodded toward the church fellowship hall, which had been transformed with the judicious use of candles, mirrors, and pearls. Connie and I had been close friends for years, and our bond was enhanced by the fact that she and her husband, Bob, were also adoptive parents. Their beautiful daughter, Brianna, had come to them from Korea, and Bri and Alex had grown up together as good friends.

"I had a lot of help," I answered, pointing in the direction of my mother. She had come out of decorating retirement to make our twenty-fifth anniversary party special for Phil and me. I looked around the room that was filled with friends and family. It didn't seem possible that Phil and I had been married for twenty-five years. Noticing Alex sitting with his cousins, I marveled that our son was growing into a handsome young man. He had become a gifted athlete and was already competing at the state level in track. His dream was to go to the Olympics someday. I had no reason to doubt it; I had seen some pretty amazing dreams come true myself. Ethan scampered around us, followed closely by Mariah, and Jonathan. Christine and I spent many days together with our four little ones. I looked around for the baby of the group, and finally saw her standing near the cake. Just as she reached up to swipe some frosting, Phil caught her up in his arms and her giggles could be heard around the room. Our beautiful daughter, Kate; today she looked like a princess with her organza dress and intricate curls.

Moving around the room, I found myself at a table with old friends that I hadn't seen in many years. As they asked about our children, I began to share some of the amazing miracles that God had performed in bringing our family together.

"You must have a lot of faith!" Donna exclaimed when I finished sharing Kate's story.

"No, just enough, I guess, when I need it," I laughed. "But really, I believe there is a reason that God has blessed us this way, beyond just completing our family." At Donna's questioning look, I explained. "A few years after Alex was born, I was reading my Bible one day, and I came across a Scripture that said, "Publish God's good works." After Ethan and Katelynn were born, I was even more convinced that God wants me to share our story with others. I believe God wants to open up the hearts of people to adoption, especially transracial adoption, in preparation for the day when there is no more abortion." Donna looked shocked, but I continued. "I know it sounds radical, but I really believe there will be a time when abortion will be stopped, at least for a while. And the Church needs to be ready and willing to receive those children with open arms and hearts. I believe God brought us our children in such amazing ways so He can show people how faithful He is to bring them the right child in the right time. And it's my privilege to tell our story to stir their faith."

As the afternoon wore on, I continued to visit with our guests, catching up on their lives and sharing ours. Finally, I found myself at a table with Christine's parents and sisters.

Jim and Nancy had retired from full-time ministry several years earlier and often traveled around the country, so I was delighted that they were in town for our celebration. As we reminisced, I reminded them that as a young bride, I had sat in their living room one Sunday afternoon and asked God to let me someday live in the house they had built. We were conscious of the intertwining of our lives; Christine and I had first grown to be dear friends, and now we had children who were biological siblings. One by one, my family started to join us at the table, and soon I had Ethan snuggled on my lap as Alex held Kate. Phil stood behind me with his hands on my shoulders. Friends had recommended that Phil and I take a cruise to commemorate our twenty-five years together, but looking around at my family, I couldn't think of a better way to celebrate our anniversary.

Christine's sisters, Jackie and Diane, began to admire

my wedding dress, which was displayed in the corner of the room.

"Dad," Diane asked Jim. "I don't remember attending Phil and Debbi's wedding. Didn't we know them back then?"

"Oh yes," Jim answered. "Phil was part of our congregation when he and Debbi met, and even though they married at her church, we were all invited to the wedding."

"But we couldn't go," Nancy added, solemnly. I thought back to that day and remembered that Jim and Nancy hadn't been at our wedding after all.

"Why not?" Jackie asked.

"Oh, we had a good reason," Jim said with a twinkle. "We had something scheduled that couldn't be changed, so we had to send our regrets."

"Well, you were Phil's pastor for goodness sake. What was so important that you couldn't attend his wedding?" Jackie seemed embarrassed by her parent's apparent social gaffe.

"Oh, I think Phil and Debbi will forgive us when we tell them what we were doing that day." Jim smiled fully now, and suddenly I sensed the presence of the Lord surrounding us.

"You see, twenty-five years ago today, on the day that Phil and Debbi were married, we were pouring the foundation for the house where they and their family live today."

The silence around the table was poignant as we each realized the importance of those words. Years ago God had laid a foundation for our family, not only of brick and mortar, but of love, commitment, and His overwhelming faithfulness. I felt Phil squeeze my shoulders, and I reached up to take his hand. We had come so far together; I couldn't wait to see where God would take us from here.

Later that afternoon, we packed up the reminders of our first twenty-five years together. Then we gathered up our three beautiful children of promise, and went home.

Chapter Twenty-Eight

Pastor Mike approached the pulpit as Phil and the worship team began to play. Several years earlier, we had been led to join Trinity church, and we were excited by the things we saw God doing there. The message that morning had been about vision, and for the first time in many months, I felt a stirring in my spirit. It wasn't that I had drifted away from God, but the demands, however welcome, of my growing family had seemed to consume most of my time and energy. Just that week I had cried out, "*God, where do I go from here?*"

Certainly I was committed to my husband and children, but recently I had sensed a longing for something more, and I wasn't sure what it was. I was reasonably certain that our family was complete, so I didn't think this was about another baby. But I had learned to listen to that tugging on my heart, and when Pastor Mike asked for anyone to come forward who wanted to have a renewed vision, I asked Alex to get his brother and sister from children's church. Then I made my way to the altar.

Making myself comfortable in a chair, I bowed my head, silently pouring out my heart to God. After a few moments, the confusion began to leave and it seemed that my thoughts began to focus on a long ago calling: Child of Promise. The words whispered in my spirit, *Child of Promise.* My heart began to pound as I considered that this might be the time to step out and declare the secrets God had been whispering to my spirit for years.

My first indication that God was going to use me to speak out about adoption had come when Alex was just six months old. I had been driving home from visiting my parents one day and was singing softly so I wouldn't disturb Alex, who was sleeping in his car seat in the back. Suddenly, sensing the presence of God with me, I was amazed at the things He began to speak to my heart concerning adoption. I sensed Him saying that He would be using adoption as a response to abortion, and that there would be a day when abortion was no longer the law of the land. I could hardly believe what I was hearing, but I knew that when that day came, the church needed to be ready with open hearts to receive these children. What the enemy had planned for evil (abortion), God was going to use for good (adoption). I also heard Him say that during that time, thousands of babies would be given to Godly parents with the purpose of raising them as warriors for the Kingdom. The very children the enemy sought to kill before birth would be part of the end time army that would ultimately bring his downfall.

My heart was also broken for the young women who faced such agonizing choices, and had to forever live with the consequences. Abortion was offered as a quick solution with no regard for the long term effects it had on their lives. From that day on, I knew that God was calling me to express His heart for adoption.

My thoughts turned to another Sunday morning, many years earlier, when Phil and I had visited a church while on vacation. That morning, the pastor had announced he would be preaching on barrenness. Of course, I was instantly aware that we were in the middle of a divine appointment, and I soaked up every truth that the minister offered concerning spiritual, and especially physical barrenness. When the sermon was finished, an altar call was given for anyone who was struggling with barrenness of any sort. I had quickly made my way to the altar, knowing that I was about to have an encounter with God. A few moments later I was approached by a woman I had never met.

"I saw you as you walked to the altar, and I sensed the Lord had something He wanted me to share with you." My heart leapt as I waited expectantly.

"God says you are already pregnant.'" Joy raced through me, until she continued.

"But not with a physical child. You are pregnant with a ministry."

I had thanked the woman as graciously as I could, all the while crying out in my heart, "No! That's not what I wanted to hear! I just want a baby!"

Now, so many years later, that memory flooded back,

and this time I accepted the words with excitement: Child of Promise, a ministry. I thought of the book I knew I was destined to write, telling about the amazing miracles God had accomplished when He formed our family. A few years after Alex was born, I had received a dream from God that confirmed that calling.

In the dream I was approached by a young woman who was very pregnant. She asked if we could talk and so we began to walk down the street together, discussing her situation. This was an unplanned pregnancy, and she was considering making a plan for adoption. She seemed to need reassurance that there would be a loving family waiting for her child. As we walked, I began to tell her our story of how God had destined Alex to come into our family. Suddenly, a woman came and inter-rupted our conversation, trying to distract the young woman. Then another interruption came and another. Finally, I looked up and saw that we were standing in front of a bookstore.

"Let's go in here, where we can talk privately," I suggested. As we entered the store I noticed a small alcove with two chairs, and that is where we went to finish our conversation.

When I woke from the dream, I sensed the Lord saying that the book I was to write would not only be for adoptive parents, but it would give hope to birthmothers as well.

Now tears wet my cheeks as God began to stir up that calling He had placed deep in my heart, for such a time as this.

"God, is this really you?" I whispered the words, then raised my head and stared at the banner hanging behind the pulpit; it was filled with words describing who we are in Christ. All of the words on the banner were dimmed, except three simple ones: *Child of Promise.* I had read those words many times in the past months, but I had never *seen* them. Now, that was all I could see, and I had my answer.

"Have you ever noticed how many families at Trinity have adopted children?" I posed the question to my friend, Connie, as we waited for the waiter to deliver our lunch. "In a congregation of about two hundred, there are nine adoptive families. That seems like a large percentage," I said. "It makes me wonder if God has a special anointing on Trinity, regarding adoption."

Connie and I had been friends for sixteen years, and it seemed like we never ran out of new and exciting things to talk about. The first time Connie and her husband, Bob, walked into the Vineyard Church, I had felt my heart begin to knit with hers. Later that morning, I had followed her to the church nursery to introduce myself and was thrilled to see her pick up her beautiful daughter, Brianna, who she explained was adopted from Korea. We had literally been through life and death together since that day, and I was eager to share my new vision with her.

"I think I'm supposed to write a book about adoption." I made the statement and held my breath.

"Well, of course you are." Connie responded. "I've never doubted that for a minute. So when will you start?" Laughing, I scooped up some of our favorite spinach and artichoke dip.

"Well, how about if I start with you," I said.

Like each adoptive family that I knew, Connie and Bob had a unique story. When their two sons, Josh and Jay, had been in elementary school, Connie and Bob had decided to adopt a baby girl from Korea. Brianna had joined her new family when she was six months old. It hardly seemed possible that Brianna was almost seventeen and Alex would soon be eighteen. It seemed like just yesterday when they were playing together in the church nursery. Now the nursery had a whole new crop of babies and children, literally from all over the world. Connie spent the afternoon encouraging me to pursue whatever I sensed God calling me to do.

And a few weeks later I found myself visiting another Trinity mom, Janel, as she described their experiences with adoption. When Mike and Janel had started attending Trinity, they had just become the adoptive parents of Noah, who had recently arrived from Korea. Now, four years later, they had added Sara, who had also been born in Korea.

"Not long after Noah was born, and we came to Trinity, I became pregnant." Janel explained. "We had already started the process to adopt again from Korea, but we had to put it on hold when we found out about the pregnancy."

Sadness flitted over Janel's face as she continued. "Then at four and a half months, I miscarried. We began the adoption process again right away, but I was dreading May 14th, which would be the anniversary of the miscarriage." Janel reached down to scoop up her daughter, Sara, into her arms. "But, God is so good! I remember thinking how wonderful it would be if we could receive our referral for our next baby on May 14th. It just seemed that it might be God's way of healing the pain of the miscarriage. But since May 14th was a Saturday, I knew that couldn't happen. I went to bed on Friday night, dreading the next day and all of the painful memories it might bring."

"The next morning, I followed my same routine. As soon as I had Noah fed, I went to the computer to check on our status. The agency had a web site that was updated each day with news about which children had been matched with adoptive families. I knew in my heart that there would be no change from the previous day—for one thing the agency was closed on Saturday. But on that, of all days, I needed to hope. And of course, that was the day God chose for us to receive our referral for Sara." Janel stopped for a moment and nestled her face in Sara's neck. "Oh, that sweet baby smell," she said with a tender smile. "You see, the referral had come the day before, but our caseworker was out of town, so it hadn't been posted. But she stopped in the office after hours and decided to update the information. Exactly one year after the miscarriage, we were matched with Sara. Isn't that just like God?"

I thought about Janel's story all the way home. It was so like God to be specific with the date. He had done it with me and countless others I knew who had adopted. It was as if He wanted to affirm that these were indeed His children, to place where and when He destined.

My heart broke when I thought of a recent conversation I had with an adoption caseworker. She had explained that they had a long list of African American birthmothers who wanted to make an adoption plan. But the agency had no families to present to them—there was no one waiting for these children. As I fell asleep that night, I thought about all of the families I knew who had been blessed by adoption. But there were still so many children that needed homes. It seemed that recently, even Hollywood had caught that vision. *Could the Church do any* less?

Chapter Twenty-Nine

Glancing at the speedometer, I slowed my pace a little. It wouldn't do to arrive at Alex's track meet with a police escort. I felt that familiar fluttering in my stomach that always arrived before every track event. It seemed almost impossible to believe that the little baby I carried from the courthouse so many years ago was now a senior in high school. It wasn't surprising that Alex's graduation party was scheduled for May 19th. The date that God had whispered to my heart eighteen years earlier seemed destined to be a special date in Alex's life forever.

Sliding my min-van into a parking place near the stadium, I hurried to grab a seat on the bench. Across the field I could see Alex warming up near the hurdles. When he had been ten years old, Alex had announced that someday he would run in the Olympics.

What had seemed like a lofty dream then was starting to come into focus as a real possibility. Alex's natural gifting, added to his hard work, had already sent him to the state competition for the past five years. He had even qualified for the National Junior Olympics the previous summer, and had earned a full tuition college scholarship for the fall. To say we were proud of him was an under-statement; but even more than his athletic and academic accomplishments, we were delighted to see his deep com-mitment to God. Alex was known as a quiet young man with a peaceful and gentle spirit—of steel. When the other athletes were partying, Alex was at the gym strengthen-ing his muscles for the next contest. Often I heard him in his room at night, playing his guitar or electric piano, practicing the latest worship songs. Alex always seemed conscious that God had a wonderful destiny planned for his life, and his childhood dream of making the Olympic team didn't seem so far-fetched anymore.

As I scanned the faces in the crowd, I searched for Phil. While I wasn't always able to attend every track event because of our two little ones, Phil never missed a meet. A moment later I spotted Phil striding across the field. Smiling up at him as he joined me, I thought about what a wonderful dad he had become.

"It's a good day," Phil said as he sat down next to me. I knew he was talking about the running conditions, but I smiled at his words. It was a good day. It seemed that after all these years, Child of Promise Ministries was about to be birthed. A few months earlier, God had spoken clearly to my heart that it was finally time. Since then, I had finished writing the book and would see it published soon. And in a few short weeks, I would begin my speaking ministry by addressing the women's group at Trinity. I had even started to pray about opening an adoption agency.

It seemed the heart of God was beating louder and louder with the call to end abortion and release the spirit of adoption to the church. In just the past few years, I had watched in awe as the Supreme Court justices had been replaced, one by one. The court appeared poised to do what no one thought could ever happen: overturn Roe V. Wade.

I was especially moved by a prophetic word that I recently read on the internet, through the Elijah List. Lou Engle, who had founded Bound4Life Ministry, had received some wonderful revelation concerning God's plan to end abortion. It seemed fitting that God would use the simple children's book, Horton Hears a Who, written by Dr. Seuss, to illustrate the heartbreak of abortion. I had also been blessed by the significance of the second book, Horton Hatches an Egg, which spoke prophetically about adoption. The call was getting louder; it was indeed time to birth Child of Promise Ministries.

That afternoon, Alex won his race, and he and Phil headed home to start dinner while I ran a few errands. As I shopped, I thought about my family waiting at home for me, and my husband, Phil, who was my best friend and partner. It seemed like just yesterday when I first saw him, strumming his guitar as he worshipped. I was so blessed to have such a strong, Christian man as my husband.

Our son, Alex, would be leaving for college soon. He had grown into a handsome young man with a heart to follow God's leading in his life. I couldn't wait to see the destiny God had planned for him.

At seven years old, Ethan was a fascinating mixture of little boy and wise old man. He had a loving spirit, an agile mind, and a smile that could melt your heart. Katelynn was the baby of the family, but she made sure she kept up with her brothers at all times. On Sunday mornings she was dressed like a little princess, but I knew that as soon as we were home she would raid Ethan's closet. Moments later she would race out the back door in torn jeans and T-shirt, with Alex's old ball cap turned backwards on her head. She loved her *Jesus songs,* as she called them, and her laugh was infectious. She especially had her dad and older brother wrapped around her little finger.

For a moment, I was transported back to that Christmas Eve so many years ago, when God had first spoken adoption into my spirit. What a journey it had been. The heartache I had carried due to infertility had been replaced by deep contentment and joy because of the precious gifts God had given us. It broke my heart to imagine that other children were waiting for families that might never come. The Church needed to be ready for the babies and children God was about to bring to them; to see them as precious gifts and to raise them for the Kingdom. It was time to tell our story, and I was excited to see what new adventures God had waiting for us as we began Child of Promise Ministries. But in the meantime, I planned to delight in each day with my own family.

An hour later, I pulled into my driveway and saw Ethan and Kate playing on the wooden swing set that Phil and Alex had built for them. Phil stood on the patio, grilling steaks; Alex was sitting in the back yard, watching his brother and sister while he played his guitar. The wind carried the voices of our two little ones as they competed to see who could swing higher.

Walking across the yard to join my family, I laughed as Ethan and Kate scrambled to be the first one off the swings. And as they raced toward me, their voices echoed two of my favorite words.

"Mommy's home!"

Adoption Resources:

Child of Promise Ministries
Debbi Migit—founder

P.O. Box 323
Groveland, Il 61535
childofpromise.net
309–264–0190

A Loving Choice Adoption Services
P.O. Box 609
Middlebury, IN 46540
1–800–321–2070

Laura Christianson,
The Adoption Decision:
15 Things You Want to Know Before Adopting.
Harvest House
ISBN: 978–0-73969–2000–1

Laura Christianson,
The Adoption Network:
Your Guide to Starting a Support System
Winepress Publishing Group
ISBN: 978–1-57921–920–4

Other recommended Ministries:
The Sara Ministry
Jen Miller-founder
www.sara-ministry.com

Bound 4 Life
Lou Engle-founder
www.bound4life.com